CLIFFS NOTES on

$4.95

HAWTHORNE'S **THE SCARLET LETTER**

Cliffs®

NOTES INC.

YOUR KEY TO THE CLASSICS

A Note to the Reader

Cliffs Notes provide you with the combined efforts of teachers, writers, and editors who've studied, taught, and analyzed what literary classics mean to literature as a whole and to you in particular. Opinions expressed in the Notes aren't rigid dogma meant to discourage your intellectual exploration. You should use them as starting points to open yourself to new methods of encountering, understanding, and appreciating literature. Acquire some knowledge about the author and the work, read a brief synopsis of the work, and then read the work itself, reviewing and consulting Cliffs Notes when necessary.

Cliffs Notes give you the basics—including such features as information about the author, social and historical backgrounds, structure and tradition of literary genres, facts about the characters, critical analyses, review questions, glossaries of unfamiliar terms, foreign phrases and literary allusions, maps, genealogies, and a bibliography to help you locate more data for essays, oral reports, and term papers.

A thorough appreciation of literature allows no short cuts. By using Cliffs Notes responsibly, reviewing past criticism of a literary work, and examining fresh points of view, you can establish a unique connection with a work of literature and can take a more active part in a key goal of education: redefining and applying classic wisdom to current and future problems.

Cliff Hillegass

THE SCARLET LETTER

NOTES

including
- *Life of the Author*
- *List of Characters*
- *Brief Plot Synopsis*
- *Chapter Summaries & Commentaries*
- *Character Analyses*
- *Critical Essays*
  Hawthorne and *The Scarlet Letter*
  Hawthorne and the Romance Tradition
  Hawthorne's Symbolism
  Hawthorne's Style
  Historical Materials and Figures
  Hawthorne and the Use of Ambiguity
- *Suggested Essay Topics*
- *Selected Bibliography*

by
Terry J. Dibble, Ph.D.
Professor of English
Milligan College
  at Milligan College, Tennessee

Cliffs Notes

INCORPORATED

LINCOLN, NEBRASKA 68501

Editor	Consulting Editor
Gary Carey, M.A.	*James L. Roberts, Ph.D.*
University of Colorado	*Department of English*
	University of Nebraska

ISBN 0-8220-1165-4
© Copyright 1988
by
Cliffs Notes, Inc.
All Rights Reserved
Printed in U.S.A.

1998 Printing

Cliffs Notes, Inc.   Lincoln, Nebraska

CONTENTS

THE SCARLET LETTER
Notes

LIFE OF THE AUTHOR

Born July 4, 1804, Nathaniel Hathorne was the only son of Captain Nathaniel Hathorne and Elizabeth Clarke Manning Hathorne. (Nathaniel added the "w" to the spelling of the family name shortly after his graduation from college in order to make the spelling of the name conform to the way it was pronounced.) Captain Hathorne died in Dutch Guiana in 1808, leaving his four-year-old son with his mother and two sisters, Elizabeth and Maria Louisa.

Following the death of Captain Hathorne, the family was forced to move in with Mrs. Hathorne's relatives, the Mannings. There they came under the close scrutiny of Grandmother Manning and two uncles, Richard and Robert Manning. It was during this period that Hawthorne's mother began to withdraw into what was later to become a lifetime of near-seclusion.

Even though Nathaniel began his early studies with Joseph E. Worcester, who became a well-known lexicographer, he was not particularly fond of school. An injury to his foot when he was nine years old allowed Nathaniel to avoid the regular schooling to which the other boys were subjected. His sister Elizabeth reported that the time at home gave him the opportunity to read Shakespeare, Spenser, and Bunyan. During this period, Mrs. Hathorne moved the small family to the banks of Sebago Lake, near the town of Raymond, Maine, where they lived on land owned by the Manning family.

Although Nathaniel was sent to school once again, his fondest memories during this period were of the times when "I ran quite wild, and would, I doubt not, have willingly run wild till this time, fishing all day long, or shooting with an old fowling piece." This idyllic life was to continue until 1819, when his Uncle Robert decided that

Nathaniel needed to return to Salem in order to continue his preparation for entrance into college.

In 1821, Nathaniel entered Bowdin College. Among his classmates were two young men who also attained fame. One, Henry Wadsworth Longfellow, became a well-known poet; the other, Franklin Pierce, became the fourteenth president of the United States. Another classmate, Horatio Bridge, was later to offer Boston publisher Samuel G. Goodrich a guarantee against loss if he would publish Hawthorne's first collection of short tales.

Hawthorne was not an outstanding student at Bowdin. He graduated in the middle of his class in 1825 and returned to his mother's house, where he spent much of the next twelve years (1825–37) in what he referred to as "this dismal chamber," an upstairs room in his mother's home on Charter Street in Salem.

Many early critics were fascinated with this twelve-year period of apparent isolation, and they speculated at length about Hawthorne's activities during that time. Recent scholars have shown that Hawthorne himself was at least partially responsible for creating the myth of the hermit-artist who labored in considerable isolation – not only from the world, but from his family as well. Although it is true that Hawthorne spent considerable time reading, writing, and poring over books of colonial history, he was not the recluse that he would have the world believe him to be. Hawthorne socialized in Salem and had a number of innocent flirtations. Rather regularly, he also used the free passage that was available on his uncle's stagecoach line in order to make summer excursions around New England. One year, he even traveled as far west as Detroit.

Hawthorne's twelve-year apprenticeship in the "chamber under the eaves" of his mother's house was not financially rewarding. He did, however, practice and then master his craft there, and in 1828, he published his first novel, *Fanshaw: A Tale,* at his own expense. Dissatisfied with the work, he later recalled the book and destroyed all the copies he could find. Then, in 1830, the *Salem Gazette* published his first story, "The Hollow of the Three Hills." By 1838, he had written more than two-thirds of the tales and sketches he was to write during his lifetime. Unfortunately, he was unable to interest a publisher in bringing out a collection of his tales before 1837, and, as a consequence, many of them were printed in newspapers, magazines, and the popular literary annuals that were published in the fall of the year and sold as genteel Christmas gifts. Since the stories in these publications were generally printed anonymously, Hawthorne gained no public notice as a writer until 1837, when Bridge backed the publication of the first volume of *Twice-Told Tales*.

Frustrated by his inability to find a publisher who would bring out a collection of his tales, Hawthorne turned to literary hack work in 1836. From March to August of that year, he worked as the editor of the *American Magazine of Useful and Entertaining Knowledge* for the salary of five hundred dollars per year. When a fire forced the magazine into bankruptcy, Hawthorne resigned and undertook, with the help of his sister Elizabeth, the task of writing a history volume for Goodrich entitled, *Peter Paley's Universal History*. Although the book was popular and Goodrich made a good profit from it, Hawthorne was paid only one hundred dollars for the work.

With the publication of *Twice-Told Tales* in 1837, Hawthorne's name was finally before the public. His modest success, however, was not to provide him with an income sufficient to support a family. Consequently, after he met Sophia Peabody in 1838 and became engaged to her in 1839, he found it necessary to seek better-paying work. In order to save money for his marriage, Hawthorne, with the help of some influential friends, secured a job as a measurer of salt and coal in the Custom House at Boston. Unhappily, his duties there tired him to the point that he was unable to produce any additional fiction during this period. Then, as a result of a change in the political party controlling the government, Hawthorne decided to resign from this position in 1841.

Still not convinced that he had adequate financial security to marry, Hawthorne invested a thousand dollars of his meager capital in the Brook Farm Community at West Roxbury. There is evidence to indicate that Hawthorne had hoped to provide a means of livelihood for himself and his bride-to-be, but the work schedule at Brook Farm left him exhausted and gave him little time to write. Finally, the work schedule, Hawthorne's lack of sympathy with the Transcendentalist viewpoint espoused by the community, and the fact that the farm appeared to be financially unsuccessful, led Hawthorne to write to Sophia: "Thou and I must form other plans for ourselves." He resigned from the community in November, 1841.

Impatient over the long engagement to Sophia and encouraged by a trip to Boston, where he reached an understanding about the rate of pay for future contributions to the *Democratic Review,* Hawthorne decided to marry. He and Sophia Peabody were married in Boston on July 9, 1842, and immediately following the ceremony, they left for Concord, Massachusetts, where they took up residence in the now-famous "Old Manse." There, Hawthorne had many of the leading Transcendentalists of the day as neighbors and associates. The most famous were Emerson, Thoreau, Fuller, and Alcott. Life at the "Old Manse" was both happy and productive. Hawthorne was able to contribute to the *Democratic Review* and to produce some of the tales which were to appear in *Mosses from an Old Manse,* published in 1846.

Financial problems, however, continued to plague the family. The birth of their first child, Una—named after the heroine of Spenser's *Faerie Queen*—led Hawthorne once again to seek government employment. With the help of his friends, Hawthorne succeeded in being appointed "Surveyor for the District of Salem and Beverly and Inspector of the Revenue for the Port of Salem." He was installed in that office on April 22, 1846, at a salary of $1,200 per year. On June 22, his son, Julian, was born. Although the new job eased the financial problems for the family, Hawthorne again found little time to pursue his writing. His experiences during this time, however, provided some of the material which he later used in the "Custom House" section of *The Scarlet Letter.*

The victory of the Whigs in the 1848 presidential election cost Hawthorne his position. It was a financial shock to the family, but the loss of the position at the Custom House provided the time necessary for him to write *The Scarlet Letter.*

The death of Hawthorne's mother on July 31, 1849, placed both emotional and financial strains on him, but with the help of money which Sophia had, unknown to Hawthorne, saved from her allowance for household expenses, he resolved to try once again to earn his living as a writer. During the next seven months, Hawthorne worked both mornings and afternoons in order to finish *The Scarlet Letter.*

The book sold well, but it was pirated by two London publishers, and thus the financial rewards were not great for Hawthorne. In addition, Hawthorne was exposed to the wrath of a number of Salemites who were angry about certain passages from the "Custom House" section of the novel. Late in May, the Hawthornes moved from Salem to the "Little Red House" in Lennox, Massachusetts, where they lived until November 21, 1851. It was there that Hawthorne made the acquaintance of Herman Melville, who was writing *Moby Dick*. Melville's dedication of the novel to Hawthorne is evidence of Hawthorne's impact on Melville.

The period at the "Little Red House" was a productive time for Hawthorne as it was here that he wrote *The House of the Seven Gables*, and he also produced other minor works that were to be published during 1851. It was here, also, that Hawthorne's second daughter, Rose, was born. Hawthorne was not happy with the climate in the Berkshires, yet it is probable that the family would have stayed there another winter, had not a dispute arisen between the owners of the house and the Hawthornes over the use of fruit from an adjoining orchard. When they were offered the use of the house of Congressman Horace Mann, Sophia's brother-in-law, the Hawthornes decided to accept the offer. They moved to West Newton, and the following year, 1852, Hawthorne published *The Blithedale Romance*, based on his experiences at Brook Farm, and *A Wonder Book for Girls and Boys*.

The Mann home was only a temporary expedient, and the Hawthornes continued to look for a permanent house, which they finally found, along with nine acres of land, in Concord, for $1,500. Bronson Alcott, the Transcendentalist writer from whom Hawthorne purchased the house, called it "The Hillside." Hawthorne objected to that name because the house stood at the base of "a steep ascent," so he renamed the place "The Wayside." The Hawthornes moved into their new home in May, 1852.

"The Wayside" was the Hawthornes' first permanent home; it even contained an elaborately decorated study, but Hawthorne wrote only two of his works there. One, *Tanglewood Tales*, was another collection designed for a young audience; the other, *A Life of Pierce*, was written as a campaign biography for his former classmate and the future president of the United States. As a result of the Pierce biography, Hawthorne was rewarded with an appointment as United States Consul at Liverpool, England.

While serving as consul, Hawthorne wrote no additional fiction. He did, however, keep a journal which later served as source material for *Our Old Home*, a collection of sketches dealing with English scenery, life, and manners published in 1863. Hawthorne remained as consul until August 31, 1857, when he resigned following the election of President Buchanan. Following his resignation, the Hawthornes moved to Italy, where he and his family lived in Rome and Florence from 1858 to 1859.

While in Italy, the Hawthornes visited art museums and toured historical sites. Hawthorne also kept a notebook which was to provide material for his final, complete work of fiction, *The Marble Faun.* Returning to England, Hawthorne finished the manuscript for *The Marble Faun;* it was published in England as *Transformation.* Then, on June 16, 1860, the Hawthornes sailed from Liverpool, bound for Boston.

The remaining years of Hawthorne's life were mixed with both pleasure and frustration. Returning to "The Wayside," Hawthorne invested in expensive renovations of the house which he could ill afford. He was constantly apprehensive because he was afraid that the illness which had afflicted Una in Rome might recur. Despite these anxieties, though, life settled into a somewhat comfortable routine, and between various social activities, Hawthorne began to work again.

By the autumn of the following year, Hawthorne was a sick man. Despite his illness, however, he went to Boston in December to attend the funeral of the wife of his old friend Pierce. By March of the following year, Sophia wrote to a friend that Hawthorne was "indeed very indisposed." In an attempt to improve his health, Hawthorne decided to take a trip to Havana with another friend, W. D. Ticknor. Bad weather prevented their sailing, so the two friends went on to Philadelphia, where Ticknor came down with pneumonia and died on April 10, 1864. Shaken by the loss of his friend, Hawthorne's health continued to decline. A month later, he decided to travel to New Hampshire with his old classmate Pierce in search of improved health. During this trip, Hawthorne died in his sleep on May 19, 1864, in Plymouth, New Hampshire. He was buried in the Sleepy Hollow Cemetery at Concord. Among his pallbearers were Longfellow, Holmes, Lowell, and Emerson. Former President Pierce accompanied Mrs. Hawthorne and the children to the funeral.

LIST OF CHARACTERS

Hester Prynne

Hester is a young English woman. She and her husband were living in Amsterdam several years before the action of the novel begins, and she was sent to the colonies by her husband, who said that he would join her shortly, as soon as business matters were settled in Amsterdam.

As the novel begins, Hester has been living in Boston for two years and has been found guilty of bearing a child by an unknown father. As punishment for her sin, she is forced to wear a scarlet *A* on the bodice of her dress and to stand on a public scaffold before Boston's townspeople.

Although Hester eventually wins acceptance by the townspeople because of her community service, it is not until after the death of her secret lover, Reverend Dimmesdale, and the marriage of her daughter that she is able to return to Boston, where she becomes a revered figure in the community, one to whom "people brought all their sorrows and perplexities, and besought her counsel." At her death, she is buried near Dimmesdale's grave.

Reverend Arthur Dimmesdale

Dimmesdale is the unmarried pastor of Hester's congregation, and he is also the father of Hester's daughter, Pearl. At the beginning of the novel, Dimmesdale reminds Hester that her refusal to name him as her fellow sinner will "tempt him – yea, compel him, as it were – to add hypocrisy to sin."

As the novel progresses, Dimmesdale justifies his decision to keep his guilty secret on the grounds that some men retain "a zeal for God's glory and man's welfare," and that in order to be of further service to his fellow creatures, he (and men like him) must, of necessity, suffer "unutterable torment." It is only when Dimmesdale recognizes the folly of this line of thought that he is able to confess his sin openly before the town and die in relative peace. Dimmesdale's secret guilt and anguish provide much of the tension throughout the novel.

Pearl

Pearl is the illegitimate daughter of Hester Prynne and the Reverend Arthur Dimmesdale. Pearl is given her symbolic name because she was, as it were, purchased at great price – "all she [Hester] had." The allusion, of course, is to the passage from the gospel of Matthew 13:45–46.

Hester soon discovers that Pearl cannot "be made amenable to rules," and she fears that Pearl's personality was formed "during that momentous period while Pearl was imbibing her soul from the spiritual world and her bodily frame from its material of earth." During the course of the novel, Pearl becomes the living manifestation of Hester's sin; Hester sees the child as "endowed with a million-fold the power of retribution for my sin!" When Hester tries to shed the scarlet *A* from her dress during her forest rendezvous with Reverend Dimmesdale, it is Pearl who insists that Hester return the scarlet *A* to her dress. Pearl receives a considerable inheritance from Chillingworth at his death, and at the end of the novel, she is rumored to be living in Europe, the wife of a member of the nobility.

Roger Chillingworth

"Chillingworth" is the pseudonym which is assumed by Hester Prynne's aged scholar-husband. After having sent Hester ahead of him to America, he suffered "grievous mishaps by sea and land" in his attempt to join her. Among those mishaps, he was held captive for a time by Indians.

Roger is recognized by Hester as she stands on the scaffold undergoing her sentence of shame. Later, in her prison cell, he convinces her to promise that she will not reveal that he is her lawful husband. He asks her to keep this vow because he does not wish to suffer "the dishonor that besmirches the husband of a faithless woman." He then vows to seek out the seducer of his wife and to observe "Heaven's own method of retribution" for that man. Chillingworth's desire for revenge and his obsession to plumb the depths of Dimmesdale's heart changes him from a caring, concerned man at the beginning of the novel to an evil fiend who dies shortly after the death of Dimmesdale.

Governor Bellingham

This actual historical figure, Richard Bellingham, arrived in Boston in 1634. He was elected governor in 1641, 1654, and 1665. As governor in this work of fiction, he witnesses Hester's punishment as she stands on the public scaffold. Later, in Chapters 7 and 8, Hester goes to Governor Bellingham's to ask that Pearl not be taken from her.

Mistress Hibbins

Another historical figure, Ann Hibbins was executed for witchcraft in 1656. In the novel, Mistress Hibbins is described as the "bitter-tempered sister" of Governor Bellingham, and Hawthorne notes that she was executed later as a witch. Because she is supposedly in league with the Black Man, the devil, she is given insight into the sins of both Hester and Arthur Dimmesdale; she even tempts both of them to become more deeply involved in their evil ways.

John Wilson

The historical figure on whom this character is based was an English-born minister who arrived in Boston in 1630. It is he who, as "the eldest clergyman of Boston," convinces Reverend Dimmesdale that he should question Hester in an attempt to convince her to reveal the name of Pearl's father. Following Hester's refusal to name Pearl's father, Wilson delivers a long sermon on the sin of adultery to the crowd that has gathered to witness Hester's punishment.

Master Brackett

He is the old jailer who brings Chillingworth to Hester while she is in prison. He also smiles and nods in recognition of Pearl and her mother as they wait for the Election Day procession to begin.

The Sexton

A minor employee of the church, he finds Reverend Dimmesdale's glove on the scaffold and returns it to him in the morning, following Dimmesdale's vigil there with Hester and Pearl. Dimmesdale lies to the sexton when questioned about having seen the starry "portent" in the sky the night before.

The Commander

As the captain of the crew of the ship on which Hester and Dimmesdale hoped to take passage, he informs Hester that another passenger will be sailing with Pearl, Dimmesdale, and her. He is, of course, referring to Hester's husband, Roger Chillingworth.

BRIEF PLOT SYNOPSIS

On a June day in 1642, a large number of people who live in the small town of Boston have gathered to witness an official act of punishment. Hester Prynne, a young woman of the community, has been found guilty of adultery, and she has been sentenced to wear a scarlet *A* on the bodice of her dress. Furthermore, she must stand on the scaffold for three hours, exposed to the scorn of her fellow townspeople.

As Hester approaches the scaffold, many of the cruel-faced women of Boston are angered by her beauty and her quiet dignity. They feel that her punishment is not sufficient for the nature of her crime, and they comment that if they had been her judge, they would have branded an *A* on her forehead – or even executed her – because of her adultery. Hester's good reputation in the past is well known, however, and it is that reputation which influenced the judges' decision to grant her some leniency.

In England, Hester's family was once wealthy, but when they lost their money, Hester's parents arranged for her to be engaged to a scholar, an older man with a slight physical deformity. After the couple were married, they lived in Amsterdam for some time before deciding to settle in the American colonies.

As the book opens, we discover that Hester arrived in Boston about two years ago. She was sent there alone, ahead of her husband, while he concluded their affairs in Amsterdam. However, Hester never heard from him after she left Amsterdam, and because he never arrived in the colonies, most people assumed that he was lost at sea. Because Hester led a quiet life until the time of her disgrace, and because she was both young and attractive – and therefore subject to great temptation – the judges decided to lighten her sentence.

Standing on the scaffold, Hester looks out over the crowd, and she notices a small, misshapen man. It is her long-lost husband. She reacts to his presence by pressing her baby to her bosom so tightly that it utters a cry of pain. When the stranger sees Hester, a "powerful emotion" darkens his face, and he turns to a townsman and asks for information about the young woman on the scaffold. He hears the story of Hester's adultery and, angry, says that the "partner of her iniquity" – that is, the man who fathered Hester's child – should be punished along with her. He vows that someday the identity of that man "will be known!"

Meanwhile, Hester is questioned by Reverend John Wilson and by the pastor of her church, Reverend Arthur Dimmesdale. Both men urge Hester to reveal the name of the father of her child – her "fellow sinner" – but Hester stubbornly refuses to do so. Frustrated, Reverend Wilson gives a long lecture on the general topic of sin, continually stressing Hester's particular violation of the moral law. Throughout the latter part of the ordeal, Hester's baby wails and screams.

After Hester is returned to her prison cell, Master Brackett, the jailer, is unable to control her nervous frenzy, and feeling that it is necessary to seek the help of a physician in order to calm both Hester and her child, he brings in Roger Chillingworth, the misshapen old physician, to administer medicinal herbs and roots to the two prisoners. Unknown to Master Brackett, of course, is the fact that Chillingworth is actually Master Prynne, Hester's missing husband.

Dismissing the jailer, Chillingworth first treats Pearl, Hester's baby. During his conversation with Hester, Chillingworth admits that he wronged her by betraying her "budding youth into a false and unnatural relation" with his decaying old age. But, he says, he had hoped that his intellect and his desire for "a household fire" would be enough to win Hester's love. Now he acknowledges his mistake and realizes that "the scale hangs fairly balanced" between the two of them. He demands, however, to know the name of the child's father. When Hester refuses to give him the name, he insists that Hester never reveal that he is her husband. If she ever does so, he warns her, he will destroy Pearl's father. Hester agrees to Chillingworth's terms, even though she suspects that she should not have done so.

Following her release from prison, Hester settles in a small thatched cottage at the edge of town, on the shore, and she begins to earn her living by doing fancy needlework. Because of her extraordinary talent with a needle, her handiwork soon becomes "the fashion." Evidence of her skill is especially apparent in the clothing which she sews for Pearl. Although Hester herself wears the somber clothes of the Puritans, Pearl's dresses are bold and richly decorated.

Living alone with Pearl, Hester is troubled by the unusual character of her daughter. As an infant, the child is fascinated by the scarlet A on her mother's dress; it is the first object which the child reaches for. As she grows older, Pearl becomes a capricious and unruly child and is hard to discipline. As a result of her conduct in the town, rumors begin to circulate that Pearl is "a demon offspring." Not surprisingly, the conservative church members suggest that Pearl be taken away from Hester.

Hester hears these rumors and fears that they may be true: Pearl may indeed be taken from her by the magistrates of the town. Therefore, Hester plans to use the opportunity of delivering a pair of embroidered gloves to Governor Bellingham in order to speak to him about her fears.

While waiting in the governor's hall, Pearl calls her mother's attention to a reflection in a suit of armor hanging on the wall. Its convex shape reflects a distorted image of the scarlet letter on Hester's bodice, making the A appear "the most prominent feature of her appearance," much to the satisfaction of Pearl. The child's perversity becomes more pronounced when Governor Bellingham and his three guests enter the hall.

Governor Bellingham sees Pearl, clad in flaming scarlet, and he asks her name, to which she replies, "Pearl"—a name wholly incongruous with her physical appearance. In the conversation which follows, the governor suggests that there is some consideration being given to taking the child away from Hester, and he suggests that one of his guests, Reverend Wilson, should question Pearl to see if she "hath had such Christian nurture as befits a child of her age."

Although Pearl has been taught the basic elements of the catechism, she refuses to answer the minister's questions, and the situation becomes desperate. When it appears that the child is about to be taken from her, Hester appeals to another of the governor's guests, Reverend Dimmesdale, who, along with Roger Chillingworth, has been watching the proceedings. Dimmesdale persuades the governor to let Hester keep the child, who seems to be strangely attracted to Dimmesdale.

As Pearl and her mother are leaving the governor's mansion, they are met by Mistress Hibbins (who, Hawthorne tell us, is later hanged for being a witch). She asks if Hester is willing to go into the forest with her that evening. Hester declines her invitation but reveals that if the magistrates had taken Pearl from her, she would have been willing to go with the witch and sign her name—in blood—in the Black Man's book.

Hester's confrontation with Governor Bellingham, as well as with Reverend Dimmesdale's defense of her right to keep Pearl, were both witnessed by Roger Chillingworth, who, since his arrival in town, has become intimately acquainted with Reverend Dimmesdale. Because Dimmesdale's health began to fail shortly after Hester was punished on the scaffold, the townspeople were happy to have Chillingworth, an old physician, take up lodgings in the same house with Dimmesdale. Being in such close contact with Dimmesdale, Chillingworth has come to know the minister's most intimate emotions, and he has begun to suspect that Dimmesdale's illness is the result of some unconfessed guilt rather than a physical affliction. As he applies psychological pressure to Dimmesdale in order to discover the secret sin that is causing the debilitating illness, Chillingworth begins to suspect that Dimmesdale is Pearl's father, and his suspicions are apparently confirmed when he examines Dimmesdale's chest one evening while Dimmesdale is sleeping.

Pulling Dimmesdale's vestment aside, Chillingworth sees something startling on the pale chest of the sleeping minister, and he bursts into "a ghastly rapture." From that moment forward, his relationship with Dimmesdale changes. He becomes "a chief actor in the minister's interior world."

Continuously tormented by his guilty conscience, Dimmesdale goes to the square where Hester was punished "seven long years earlier." As he stands on the scaffold performing his "mockery of penitence," he sees Reverend Wilson returning from the "death chamber of Governor Winthrop," where he has been praying at the dying man's bedside. A little later, Hester, who has also been watching at the same deathbed, comes by with little Pearl. He calls them onto the scaffold with him, acknowledging that they have both been there before, but that he lacked the courage to be there with them at that time. He admits his guilt to them, but he refuses Pearl's request to stand with them the following day.

Suddenly, Dimmesdale notices a meteor forming what appears to be a gigantic A in the sky, and simultaneously he sees little Pearl pointing her finger toward the figure of Roger Chillingworth, who has been watching them on the scaffold.

Later, after Hester and Pearl stood with Dimmesdale on the scaffold, Hester is so shocked by Dimmesdale's rapidly deteriorating condition that she feels something must be done to remedy the situation. Consequently, she decides to talk to Chillingworth in order to obtain a release from her vow of silence.

One afternoon, she sees Chillingworth gathering herbs, and sending Pearl away, she tells the old physician that she is going to tell Dimmesdale about her promise to Chillingworth and warn him against

Chillingworth's evil intentions. She also tells Chillingworth that his obsession for revenge is affecting him – as well as Dimmesdale – but Chillingworth says that he cannot pardon Dimmesdale, and he goes back to gathering herbs.

Several days later, Hester learns that Dimmesdale will be returning from a visit to the Reverend Eliot, who has been a missionary to the Indians. Meeting Dimmesdale in the forest on his way home, she confesses to him that Chillingworth is her husband, and she warns Dimmesdale that he should be aware of the old physician's desire for revenge. As a result of their conversation, Hester convinces Dimmesdale to leave Boston in secret and take passage on a ship which is anchored in the harbor. Hoping to begin life anew, Hester removes the scarlet A, and she and Dimmesdale make plans to sail for England.

Apparently renewed by this decision, Dimmesdale seems to gain new energy. Therefore, Hester calls Pearl to her side so that she too can share in the delightful news, but the child refuses to cross the brook which separates her from her mother and the minister. It is not until Hester replaces the scarlet A on her dress that Pearl agrees to join them.

Returning to town, Dimmesdale is seized by a number of irrational desires: to utter blasphemies to one of his church deacons, shatter the hopes of an elderly matron, and blight the innocence of a young girl. He talks to Mistress Hibbins, and she suggests that he has made a visit to the forest; she also implies that very soon he will walk into the forest with her. Terrified that he has sold himself to the devil, Dimmesdale rushes back to his room, where he begins feverish preparations for the sermon which he is to deliver on Election Day, the day when the new governor is to be installed in office.

On Election Day morning, Hester and Pearl appear in the town square to observe the parade. Hester warns Pearl that she is not to expect Dimmesdale to take any notice of them and that Pearl is not to greet him. While they are waiting for the parade to begin, the captain of the ship on which Hester has arranged passage to Bristol informs her that there will be an additional passenger going with them: the additional passenger will be Roger Chillingworth, whom she sees across the square, smiling with "secret and fearful meaning."

As the procession passes Hester on its way to the church, she notices that Dimmesdale is so lost in thought that he takes no notice of her and Pearl. She even begins to realize "that there could be no real bond between the clergyman and herself."

Following Dimmesdale's sermon, which the crowd declares to be one of the most inspired sermons they have ever heard, the procession leaves the church. Dimmesdale walks as though he were in a trance. He totters once and almost falls, and Reverend Wilson offers an arm in support, but Dimmesdale refuses it and walks onward.

Seeing Hester and Pearl at the foot of the scaffold, he turns toward them. Chillingworth attempts to prevent Dimmesdale from doing anything unexpected, but Dimmesdale declares that with God's help, he will escape the power of his physician. At Dimmesdale's request, Hester helps him ascend the scaffold, where he stands with her and Pearl. There, he confesses to the astonished crowd that he is Pearl's father, and with a "convulsive motion," he tears the ministerial band from his chest. He states that now, revealed for all to see, is the evidence of his sin. Then he collapses and sinks to the platform. Later, witnesses swear that they saw a stigmata in the form of a scarlet *A* upon his chest.

Following Dimmesdale's death, Hester decides to leave Boston. Chillingworth, no longer having Dimmesdale as the object of his bitter revenge, dies shortly. At his death, he wills Pearl a great deal of money, which makes her a wealthy young woman. Several years later, Hester leaves England and returns to Boston. She becomes a person to whom other women turn for solace during their times of trouble. When she dies, she is buried near the grave of Dimmesdale, but not so close that their dust can mingle. A simple slate tombstone serves for both graves.

SUMMARIES AND COMMENTARIES

The Custom House

This long essay, functioning as a preface to the novel, was originally published with the novel, even though it does not seem to be an integral part of the story. In fact, the only direct link between this essay and the novel is the passage in which Hawthorne tells of having discovered, in the Salem Custom House, the faded scarlet *A* and the parchment foolscap sheets containing the facts which he says he used as the basis for this novel.

It is almost certain that Hawthorne made up the story of his "discovery," right down to the letter A with each leg "precisely three inches and a quarter in length," as a way of giving his novel an air of historical truth. However, neither the letter A nor the foolscap has ever been seen.

Furthermore, Hawthorne, in his story "Endicott and the Red Cross," published some nine years before he took his position in the Salem Custom House, used the incident of a woman who was forced to wear the letter A on her breast. Like Hester (the heroine of *The Scarlet Letter*), this woman also "embroidered the fatal token in scarlet cloth with golden thread and the nicest art of needlework."

Although the connection between this preface and the novel is a slight and artificial one, the Custom House essay is interesting and valuable in its own right. In its reference to Hawthorne's ancestors, it provides a reason for his intense interest in the Puritan period. As a piece of autobiography, it reveals a satiric side of Hawthorne which is not reflected in the somber novel which follows it.

The preface is also proof that Hawthorne was not merely a morbid and solitary brooder over sin, but a citizen with some experience in practical affairs and some interest in contemporary politics. It demonstrates, in his sketch of the Collector ("our gallant old General"), Hawthorne's emotional response to his fellow human beings, and, in his caricature of the Inspector (who "possessed no power of thought, no depth of feeling, no troublesome sensibilities"), Hawthorne's talent for creating biting wit is evident. But, most important, Hawthorne tells us about the Surveyor (Hawthorne himself), his emotional reactions to his position and the loss of it.

1. THE PRISON-DOOR

Summary

This chapter is concerned only with setting the scene of the novel in seventeenth-century Boston, where a throng of drably dressed Puritans stands before the weatherbeaten wooden prison. In front of the prison lies an unsightly plot of weeds, and beside it grows a wild rosebush.

Commentary

Here, Hawthorne effectively sets the mood for the "tale of human frailty and sorrow" which is to follow. The rust and decay and ugliness foreshadow the gloom of the novel. The two landmarks mentioned, the prison and the cemetery, point to the themes of punishment and death, which will be combined in the climax of the story. And the rosebush, its beauty such a striking contrast to all that surrounds it, is held out as an invitation to find "some sweet moral blossom" in the tragic, ensuing story.

2. THE MARKET-PLACE

Summary

As the Puritans wait for some public punishment, the women self-righteously and viciously (with one exception) discuss the "hussy," Hester Prynne, and her sin. Hester, proud and beautiful, emerges from the prison, wearing an elaborately embroidered scarlet letter *A* (standing for "adultery") on her breast, and carrying a three-month-old infant in her arms. She is led through the cold and unsympathetic crowd to the scaffold of the pillory. Standing alone on the scaffold, she dreams of her past life in England and on the Continent—first, her life in her father's home, and, then, her life with her husband, a "misshapen scholar." Suddenly becoming aware of the stern faces looking up at her, Hester painfully realizes her present position of shame and punishment.

Commentary

Although we actually meet only Hester and Pearl (her infant daughter) in this chapter, Hawthorne begins his characterization of all four of his major characters. First, he describes Hester physically, and then he tells us about her background. We witness her combination of pride and shame, and then we see Pearl, the symbol of Hester's sin. We hear Pearl symbolically cry out when her mother fiercely clutches her at the end of the chapter.

Although the irony of Arthur Dimmesdale's relationship to Hester is not yet apparent, we obtain our first hint of his nature and his grief through the comments of one of the women assembled near the prison. She says that "the Reverend Master Dimmesdale . . . takes it very grievously to heart that such a scandal should have come upon his congregation."

And, although Roger Chillingworth is not yet named, we are given a rather full characterization of the man through Hester's recollections of him. He is the "misshapen scholar" who is Hester's legal husband.

The chapter also contains a description of the Puritan society and reveals Hawthorne's critical attitude toward it (inspired perhaps by the guilt which he felt for his two ancestors mentioned in the preface). The cold, smug, holier-than-thou attitude of the "goodwives" who condemn Hester is frightening – especially when we hear them suggest more violent torture for Hester. This scene vividly dramatizes what Hawthorne found objectionable about early American Puritanism. Yet, Hawthorne avoids over-generalizing here by including the good-hearted young wife in this scene. Her soft remarks of sympathy for Hester's suffering contrast sharply with the comments of the majority of the women.

In technique, the chapter is a sign of things to come. The somewhat heavy historical narrative, occasionally interrupted by Hawthorne's comments, and the employment of such symbols as the beadle, the letter, and Pearl – these techniques are all typical of Hawthorne's method in this novel.

3. THE RECOGNITION

Summary

Hester sees a small, rather deformed man in the company of an Indian on the outskirts of the crowd. On recognizing him, she clutches Pearl fiercely to her bosom. Meanwhile, the man, a stranger to Boston, recognizes Hester and is struck by horror.

Inquiring of a man in the crowd, he hears that Hester was sent ahead from Europe by her scholarly husband, who was to follow her; she has been in Boston for two years without any word from that learned gentleman. Because of these circumstances, she is not being executed for her sin of adultery with the unidentified father of the baby which she holds, but she will be forced to stand on the scaffold for three hours. In addition, she will have to wear the symbolic letter *A* for the rest of her life.

The deformed stranger tells the man in the crowd that he has "met with grievous mishaps by sea and land" and has been "long held in bonds among the heathen-folk" (Indians), but he was finally released from his captivity. Upon parting, he remarks, "It irks me . . . that the partner of her iniquity should not, at least, stand on the scaffold by her side. But he will be known! — he will be known! — he will be known!"

As Hester stands on the scaffold, filled with dread at the thought of meeting the man whom she saw on the outskirts of the crowd, the Reverend Mr. John Wilson, Boston's oldest and most famous minister, addresses her from an overlooking balcony, where Governor Bellingham and several other dignitaries sit, observing her punishment. The grizzled old churchman publicly calls upon Hester's pastor, the young Reverend Mr. Arthur Dimmesdale, to plead with Hester to reveal her partner in sin.

Looking straight into Hester's eyes, and in a voice "tremulously sweet, rich, deep, and broken," the pale young minister complies, concluding: "Take heed how thou deniest to him — who, perchance, hath not the courage to grasp it for himself — the bitter, but wholesome, cup that is now presented to thy lips!"

Despite the passion of Dimmesdale's appeal, followed by harsher demands from the Reverend Mr. Wilson, and from a cold, stern voice in the crowd (presumably that of the deformed stranger), Hester steadfastly refuses to name the father of her child. After a long and tedious sermon by the Reverend Mr. Wilson, during which Hester tries ineffectively to quiet the wailings and screams of her baby, she is led back to prison. "It was whispered, by those who peered after her, that the scarlet letter threw a lurid gleam along the dark passageways of the interior."

Commentary

Here, the other two principal characters of the novel make their first appearance, and the tensions of the story begin to develop. The deformed stranger who so terrifies Hester is "Roger Chillingworth" (the pseudonym he has chosen for himself); in reality, he is Roger Prynne, the husband whom Hester was remembering in the previous chapter. Now, as Chillingworth, his vow — "But he will be known!" — will dominate his actions from this chapter forward.

The other principal character in this scene is the young Reverend

Mr. Dimmesdale, who pleads with Hester to name the father of her infant daughter. Dimmesdale is the father of Pearl. This fact makes his passionate appeal one of the richest passages of irony in the novel. The careful student should read Dimmesdale's speech again, noting the strong undercurrent of personal meaning in Dimmesdale's public remarks.

4. THE INTERVIEW

Summary

Back in her prison cell, Hester is in a state of nervous frenzy, and Pearl is writhing in convulsions of pain. That evening, the jailer brings a "physician" to the cell. He is announced as "Roger Chillingworth," and he is, as we have noted, Hester's husband, the man in the crowd whose presence so alarmed Hester.

Hester fears Chillingworth's intentions, but he gives Pearl some medicine and, almost immediately, her pain is eased and she falls asleep. Clearly, Hester still fears him, but she is persuaded to drink a sedative which he has prepared. Afterward, the two sit and talk intimately and sympathetically, each of them accepting a measure of blame for the situation which developed.

Chillingworth, the injured husband, seeks no revenge against Hester, but he is determined to discover the man who violated his marriage: "He bears no letter of infamy wrought into his garment, as thou dost; but I shall read it on his heart."

Chillingworth then makes what, on the surface, appears to be a reasonable request. He says that if Hester is going to conceal the identity of her lover, then she must also keep Chillingworth's identity a secret. He promises not to take the life of her lover, or damage his reputation, if Hester will swear not to reveal that he, Chillingworth, is her husband. But he warns her that if she fails to keep the secret, then she should fear for her lover's safety. Hester takes an oath to keep Chillingworth's identity a secret, although she expresses the fear that her vow of silence may prove the ruin of her soul. To this, Chillingworth ominously replies, "Not thy soul . . . No, not thine!"

Commentary

This is a very dramatic chapter. Hawthorne does not summarize or discuss the actions of his characters, telling the reader what to think. Instead, he puts Hester and Chillingworth together and lets us learn about their attitudes and their relationship to one another by listening to them talk. The chapter is also especially important to our understanding of Chillingworth. We see what he has been, as well as what he is to become. We can sympathize with the lonely, gentle scholar who has been robbed of his wife, but we can see the element of his future self-destruction in his grim determination to discover the man who has offended him.

Of Hester, we learn that she has never pretended to love her husband, but that she deeply loves the man whom Chillingworth has vowed to punish. Ironically, it is Hester's concern for Dimmesdale, more than her sense of obligation to Chillingworth, that persuades her to promise never to reveal that Chillingworth is her husband. This promise will make both Hester and her lover, Arthur Dimmesdale, suffer later in the book.

5. HESTER AT HER NEEDLE

Summary

Hester's term of imprisonment is ended. She is now free to go anywhere in the world. Yet, she does not leave Boston; she chooses to move into a small thatched cottage by the sea, on the outskirts of town. During the following months, Hester supports herself and Pearl through her skill as a seamstress. Her work is in great demand among the fashionable women of the town—for every occasion except a wedding.

Despite the popularity of her sewing, however, Hester is a complete social outcast, the target of vicious abuse by the "respectable" women and the thoughtless children of the community. Hester takes their abuse patiently, but she does not pray for her enemies—"lest, in spite of her forgiving aspirations, the words should stubbornly twist themselves into a curse."

Commentary

In sharp contrast to the preceding chapter, Hawthorne employs not one word of dialogue here. Instead, Hawthorne summarizes many months of Hester's life, explaining Hester's situation to the reader. The chief function of this chapter is to show Hester undergoing penance for her sin of adultery. It is important to note that she goes beyond the letter of the law. For example, she stays in this atmosphere of torture when she could leave, and she dresses herself in the coarsest and most somber attire when her natural taste is for the rich and beautiful. It is also important to note that, despite Hester's apparent humility and her refusal to strike back at the community, she resents and inwardly rebels against the viciousness of her Puritan persecutors.

6. PEARL

Summary

During her first three years, Hester's daughter, whom she named "Pearl" (an allusion to the biblical pearl "of great price"), grows into a physically beautiful, vigorous, and graceful little girl. She is radiant in the rich and elaborate dresses which Hester sews for her.

Inwardly, however, Pearl possesses a character "whose elements were perhaps beautiful and brilliant, but all in disorder." She shows an unusual depth of mind, coupled with a fiery passion which Hester is incapable of controlling, either with kindness or with threats. Pearl shows a love of mischief and a disrespect for authority, which frequently reminds Hester of her own sin of passion.

Hester and Pearl are constant companions, both of them being excluded from the circle of "respectable" society. When she is on walks with her mother, Pearl occasionally finds herself surrounded by the curious children of the village. She does not attempt to make friends with them, though; instead, she pelts them with stones and violent words. Pearl's only companion in her playtime is her imagination.

Significantly, in Pearl's games of make-believe, she never creates friends. She creates only enemies – Puritans whom she pretends to destroy. But the object which most captures her imagination is the scarlet letter A on her mother's breast. Years ago, as a tiny baby, Pearl grasped for that letter; now she pelts the letter with wild flowers. It seems to Hester as though Pearl is possessed by a fiend – an impression strengthened when Pearl denies having a Heavenly Father, and then laughingly demands that Hester tell her where she "came from."

Commentary

This is a companion chapter to the previous chapter, and its method of summarizing a three-year time span is much the same. The chief function of the chapter is to solidify the impression of Pearl – the mischievous and almost unworldly child whose uncontrollable passion reflects the sinful passion which led to her birth.

Yet, the portrayal of Pearl is perhaps not so unrealistic as some critics charge. Exceptional intelligence, inherited emotional tendencies, and abnormal environment may, taken together, satisfactorily explain most of her behavior. You should note that the interpretation of Pearl's behavior as almost supernatural, or fiendish, takes place primarily in Hester's mind. As Hawthorne states it, in raising the question of the "little, laughing image of a fiend" which appears to peep out of Pearl: "Whether it peeped or no, her mother so imagined it."

The lonely companionship of Hester and Pearl, and the deep love which Hester feels for this child whom she cannot understand and whom she half-fears, add to the pathos of the story. In considering the ideas of the book, one must note the disturbing irony of Hawthorne's contrast between the Puritan community's treatment of Hester for her sin and God's treatment of her:

> Man had marked this woman's sin by a scarlet letter, which had such potent and disastrous efficacy that no human sympathy could reach her, save it were sinful like herself. God, as a direct consequence of the sin which man thus punished, had given her a lovely child, whose place was on that same dishonored bosom, to connect her parent for ever with the race and descent of mortals, and to be finally a blessed soul in heaven!

Hawthorne obviously does not think that Hester's sin is unforgivable in the eyes of God. Yet, neither Hawthorne nor Hester views the sin lightly:

> She knew that her deed had been evil; she could have no faith, therefore, that its result would be for good.

7. THE GOVERNOR'S HALL

Summary

Hester has heard that certain influential citizens feel that it would be better for both Hester and Pearl if Pearl were taken away from her. Alarmed, Hester sets out with Pearl for Governor Bellingham's mansion to deliver some gloves which he ordered. More important, however, Hester plans to plead for the right to keep her daughter.

Pearl has been especially dressed for the occasion in an elaborate scarlet dress, embroidered with gold thread so that she represents perfectly the scarlet letter on Hester's breast. Pearl is "the very brightest little jet of flame that ever danced upon the earth." When she is taunted by a group of Puritan children, she shows a temper as fiery as her appearance, driving the children off with her screams and threats.

Reaching the Governor's large, elaborate, stuccoed frame dwelling, Hester and Pearl are admitted by a bondsman who tells them that the governor is busy with a "godly minister or two" and a "leech" (a Colonial term for a doctor, or a physician).

Inside the heavy oak hall, which is described in detail by Hawthorne, Hester and Pearl stand before Governor Bellingham's suit of armor. In its curved, polished breastplate, Hester's scarlet A is magnified so that she seems to be hidden behind it. Pearl's customary mischievous grin is also magnified and distorted. In fact, Hester is so startled by the imp-like image of Pearl that she leads her to a bow-window so that she can look out at the roses while waiting for the governor.

Pearl, however, begins crying because she wants one of the red roses growing in the garden. Meanwhile, a small group of men approaches. Pearl gives one last defiant scream, then becomes quiet out of curiosity about the men who are coming down the path.

Commentary

In addition to preparing the way for the dramatic and crucial interview of the next chapter, this chapter displays Hawthorne's imagination in developing his symbols. The scarlet A, a simple and rather unimaginative symbol in itself, is strengthened by two striking variations: the magnified A in the breastplate and Pearl as a living version of the scarlet symbol.

The characterizations of Hester and Pearl are also focused on in this chapter. Pearl's almost fiendish qualities are made more vivid, both through her behavior and through her appearance in the breast-plate. Hester's proud and defiant acceptance of her punishment is demonstrated in her deliberately dressing Pearl as a crimson symbol of that sin.

In addition, the chapter is worth noting for its description of the interior of Governor Bellingham's mansion—the only such interior description in the novel.

8. THE ELF-CHILD AND THE MINISTER

Summary

The group of men approaching Hester and Pearl include Governor Bellingham, the Reverend John Wilson, the Reverend Arthur Dimmes-dale, and Roger Chillingworth, who since the story's opening has been living in Boston as Arthur Dimmesdale's friend and personal physician.

The governor, shocked at Pearl's vain and immodest costume, challenges Hester's fitness to raise the child in a Christian way. He asks Reverend Mr. Wilson to test Pearl's knowledge of the catechism. Although Hester has taught Pearl much more about religion than most other three-year-olds would normally know, Pearl deliberately pre-tends ignorance. In answer to the very first question—"Who made thee?"—Pearl replies that she was not made, but that she was "plucked . . . off the bush of wild roses that grew by the prison door."

Horrified, the governor and Mr. Wilson are ready to take Pearl immediately. Hester protests that God gave Pearl to her and that she will not give her up. She appeals to Dimmesdale to speak up for her.

Looking pale and holding his hand over his heart, Dimmesdale does speak—so eloquently, in fact, that he persuades the governor and Mr. Wilson that Hester should be allowed to keep Pearl, whom God has given her as both a blessing and a reminder of her sin.

Chillingworth, who has been smiling slyly, remarks, "You speak, my friend, with a strange earnestness." Pearl, momentarily solemn, caresses Dimmesdale's hand and receives from the minister a furtive kiss on the head. As she skips away, Chillingworth raises the question, "Would it be beyond a philosopher's research, think ye, gentlemen, to analyze that child's nature and from its make and mould, to give a shrewd guess at the father?"

Leaving the mansion, Hester is approached by Mistress Hibbins (Governor Bellingham's sister, who was actually executed as a witch in 1656). Hester refuses the woman's invitation to a midnight meeting of witches in the forest: "I must tarry at home, and keep watch over my little Pearl. Had they taken her from me, I would willingly have gone with thee into the forest, and signed my name in the Black Man's book too, and that with mine own blood!"

Commentary

For the first time since the opening scene on the scaffold, Hawthorne brings together his four major characters in this important and dramatic chapter. He also includes representatives of the Church, the State, and the World of Darkness. Note, too, that underneath the surface action, Hawthorne gives us several strong hints concerning the complex relationships of his characters. In Hester's appealing to Dimmesdale for help, in Pearl's solemnly caressing his hand, and in the minister's answering kiss lie solid hints that Dimmesdale is Pearl's father.

In addition, Dimmesdale's weakened condition and his obvious nervousness suggest how terribly he has been suffering with his concealed guilt. Also, the fact that Chillingworth is Dimmesdale's personal physician and supposed friend provides him with an opportunity to apply psychological pressure on the minister, hoping to make him bare his soul. Chillingworth's comment on Dimmesdale's strange earnestness, and his mentioning the possibility of "a shrewd guess at the father" suggest that he may already have decided on Dimmesdale's guilt.

The change noted by Hester in Chillingworth's physical appearance, now more ugly and dark and misshapen, is a hint that in Chillingworth's desire for revenge, he is becoming possessed by evil. Finally, Hester's conversation with Mistress Hibbins shows how completely dependent Hester has become on Pearl, the child of her illicit love affair with Dimmesdale.

9. THE LEECH

Summary

Since first appearing in the community, Chillingworth has been well received by the townspeople, not only because they can use his services as a physician, but also because of his special interest in their ailing clergyman, Arthur Dimmesdale. In fact, some of the Puritans now even view it as a special act of Providence that a man of Chillingworth's knowledge should have been "dropped," as it were, into their community just when their beloved young minister's health seemed to be failing. And, although Dimmesdale protests that he needs no medicine and is prepared to die if it is the will of God, he agrees to put his health in Chillingworth's hands.

The two men begin spending much time together and, finally, at Chillingworth's suggestion, they move into the same house, where, although they have separate apartments, they move back and forth freely. Then gradually, some of the townspeople, without any real evidence except for the growing appearance of evil in Chillingworth's face, begin to develop suspicions about the doctor. Rumors about his past and suggestions that he practices "the black art," with fire brought from hell, gain some acceptance.

Many of the townspeople also believe that, rather than being in the care of a Christian physician, Arthur Dimmesdale is in the hands of Satan or one of his agents, given God's permission to struggle with the minister's soul for a time. But, despite the look of gloom and terror in Dimmesdale's eyes, all of them have faith that Dimmesdale's strength is certain to bring him victory over his tormentor.

Commentary

This is another of the slow-moving chapters in which Hawthorne brings us up to date on the lives of his characters. It develops fully what was only hinted at in the more dramatic, preceding chapter — that is, it focuses on the dangerous relationship between Chillingworth and Dimmesdale. The chapter also makes clear the satanic metamorphosis that is taking place in Chillingworth's character, which Hawthorne will present more dramatically in the following chapter.

10. THE LEECH AND HIS PATIENT

Summary

Chillingworth began his "investigation" into the identity of Pearl's father with the attitude of a judge seeking truth and justice. He has changed, however. Now, he has become fiercely obsessed by his search into Dimmesdale's heart. He is frequently discouraged in his attempts to pry loose Dimmesdale's secret, but he always returns to his "digging" with all his intelligence and passion.

In one conversation with Dimmesdale, he raises the question of why a man would be willing to carry "secret sins" to his grave rather than confess them during his lifetime. Dimmesdale reminds Chillingworth that most men do confess their sins and, as a result, they are granted peace and well-being. He adds, however, that other men do not confess their sins because of the "constitution of their nature"; if certain men confessed their sins, he says, these men in question would be revealed to the world as "sinful," and they could no longer do God's work on earth.

Chillingworth quickly attacks this excuse for concealing sin. He remarks, "Wouldst thou have me to believe, O wise and pious friend, that a false show can be better – can be more for God's glory, or man's welfare – than God's own truth? Trust me, such men deceive themselves!"

Instead of replying, Dimmesdale changes the subject.

Just then, Hester Prynne and Pearl are seen through the open window, passing the adjacent graveyard. Pearl, in one of her mischievous moods, skips from grave to grave, dances on a broad tombstone, and then arranges prickly burrs around the scarlet *A* on her mother's bosom.

As Dimmesdale and Chillingworth discuss Pearl's "abnormal" nature, Pearl hears their voices. Looking up at the window, she laughingly throws a burr at Dimmesdale, then calls to her mother, "Come away, or yonder old Black Man will catch you! He hath got hold of the minister already." Watching Hester depart, Dimmesdale agrees with Chillingworth that Hester is better off with her sin publicly displayed than she would be with it concealed.

Chillingworth then renews his probing of Dimmesdale's conscience, suggesting that he can never cure Dimmesdale as long as the minister conceals anything. Finally, Dimmesdale says that his sickness is a "sickness of the soul," and, passionately crying out that he will not reveal his secret to "an earthly physician," he says, "I commit myself to the one Physician of the soul! . . . But who art thou, that meddlest in this matter? – that dares thrust himself between the sufferer and his God?"

Dimmesdale rushes from the room, and Chillingworth smiles at his success.

One day, not long afterward, Chillingworth finds Dimmesdale asleep in a chair. Pulling aside the minister's vestment (church robe), he stares at Dimmesdale's chest. What he sees there causes "a wild look of wonder, joy, and horror," and he does a spontaneous dance of ecstasy.

Commentary

In contrast to the preceding chapter, this chapter allows the reader to witness Chillingworth's diabolical determination to increase the painful inner suffering of young Arthur Dimmesdale. The chapter also gives us the best insight yet into the nature of Dimmesdale's tortured battle with himself. Clearly, he is wasting away from all the internal struggle within his soul, and yet he still cannot confess that he had an affair with Hester and that Pearl is his child. It should be noted that Dimmesdale tries to find some justification for his silence, but in the face of Chillingworth's truth and accusations, he wilts.

Nowhere does Chillingworth appear more horribly vicious than here, in this chapter, as he goads Dimmesdale and then gloats over the weakened minister's anguish. Yet Hawthorne, apparently in an effort to keep the reader from viewing Chillingworth as merely a monstrous force of evil, reminds us that Chillingworth had once been a kindly, pure, and righteous man. Chillingworth *did not choose* the path of evil. Rather, "a terrible fascination, a kind of fierce, though still calm, necessity seized the old man within its grip, and never set him free again until he had done all its bidding."

Chillingworth is thus a victim of "necessity," just as surely as Dimmesdale is a victim of his own passion.

The spectacular but mysterious reference to Dimmesdale's chest, at the end of the chapter, is an important "clue" which we should remember when we reach Chapter 23.

11. THE INTERIOR OF A HEART

Summary

Feeling that he is in full possession of Dimmesdale's secret, Chillingworth begins his unrelenting torture of the minister, subtly tormenting him by comments designed to trigger fear and agony. Dimmesdale does not realize Chillingworth's motives, but he nonetheless comes to fear and abhor him. He is confused, though, and feels that his feeling of abhorrence may come from the impurity of his own heart.

Ironically, as Dimmesdale's suffering becomes more painful and his body grows weaker, his popularity among the congregation grows stronger. His own suffering enables him to sympathize with the sins and the sufferings of others and lends a quiet eloquence to his sermons. The church members, not knowing of his terrible guilt, adore him as a "miracle of holiness." Such mistaken adoration, however, further tortures Dimmesdale and brings him often to the point of making a public confession that he is Pearl's father. His vague assertions of his own sinful nature are taken by his parishioners as further evidence of his holiness.

Because Dimmesdale is incapable of confessing that he was Hester's lover and that he is Pearl's father – the one act necessary to his salvation – he substitutes self-punishment. He beats himself with a bloody whip (while laughing bitterly) and keeps frequent all-night vigils during which his mind is plagued by frightening visions. On one such night while he is seeking peace, Dimmesdale dresses carefully in his clerical clothes.

Commentary

The focus of this chapter is on Dimmesdale's painful agony, as he writhes beneath the burden of guilt because he is powerless to confess. At this point, Hawthorne makes two additions to the plot: first, we have an indication that Chillingworth no longer has doubts about the minister's guilt; thus, he has undertaken a planned (and successful) campaign to wreak vengeance on the man who seduced his wife and fathered a child by her. Second, we have a specific statement about the methods and degrees of Dimmesdale's own self-punishment.

Hawthorne's irony is evident again in the clever paradox of Dimmesdale's futile attempts at public confession. The more that Dimmesdale asserts his own sinfulness, the holier his congregation believes him to be. Dimmesdale is aware that his inadequate confessions are being misunderstood; in fact, he is consciously taking advantage of that misunderstanding: "The minister well knew – subtle, but remorseful hypocrite that he was! – the light in which his vague confession would be viewed." Thus, his sin is compounded by his actions during his period of struggle.

Hawthorne seems eager to make sure that sympathy for Dimmesdale's suffering does not blind the reader to the fact that the minister is a sinner whose troubles are largely of his own making. At the same time, although Chillingworth appears more evil than ever in this chapter, Hawthorne inserts a sentence to keep the reader from viewing Chillingworth as an inhuman personification of evil: Chillingworth, he says, is a "poor, forlorn creature . . . more wretched than his victim."

12. THE MINISTER'S VIGIL

Summary

After leaving the house, Dimmesdale walks to the weather-stained scaffold where, seven years ago, Hester Prynne stood, holding Pearl. Now, in the damp, cool air of the cloudy May night, Dimmesdale mounts the steps while the town sleeps. Realizing the mockery of his being able to stand there now, safe and unseen, where he should have stood seven years ago before the townspeople, Dimmesdale is overcome by a self-hatred so terrible that it causes him to cry aloud into the night. Governor Bellingham and Mistress Hibbins both look out from their windows, but the minister remains unseen.

As Dimmesdale becomes calmer, he sees Reverend Mr. Wilson approaching, carrying a lantern. Wilson has just left the deathbed of Governor Winthrop, and as he passes near the scaffold, Dimmesdale barely resists a strong impulse to speak.

Still safe, Dimmesdale finds his tired mind dreaming up grimly humorous visions of what might happen if the cold, damp air should make him too stiff to get down off the scaffold. He imagines Governor Bellingham, Mistress Hibbins, Mr. Wilson, Hester, and the respectable members of his congregation finding him the next morning, half-frozen and ashamed. The vision makes him laugh, and as he does, he hears the eerie, answering laugh of a child.

Calling out to the voice, Dimmesdale discovers Hester and Pearl, who are also returning from Governor Winthrop's deathbed. They mount the scaffold, and the three of them stand hand-in-hand, Hester and Dimmesdale linked by Pearl, the product of their love and the symbol of their sin.

Twice, Pearl asks Dimmesdale if he will stand there with them at noon the next day, and when the minister says *No,* Pearl laughs and tries to pull away from him. Dimmesdale then says that he will stand there with them on "the great judgment day." As he speaks, a strange light in the sky illuminates the scaffold and its surroundings. Looking up, Dimmesdale seems to see in the sky a dull red light in the shape of an immense letter *A.*

At the same instant, Dimmesdale is aware that Pearl is pointing toward Roger Chillingworth, who stands nearby, grimly smiling up at the three people on the scaffold. Overcome with terror, Dimmesdale asks Hester about the true identity of Chillingworth, this man whom he so fears and hates.

Remembering her promise to Chillingworth, Hester is silent, but Pearl, pretending to tell Dimmesdale about Chillingworth's true identity, whispers some gibberish in his ear. Then she laughs at the joke she has played because Dimmesdale would not promise to stand on the scaffold with her and her mother the next day.

Chillingworth approaches and explains that he just happened to be passing by on his way home from attending Governor Winthrop. He chides Dimmesdale for his strange behavior, then leads him away.

The next morning, a Sunday, Dimmesdale preaches one of his finest sermons. Afterward, the sexton startles the minister by returning one of his gloves, which was found on the scaffold. ("Satan dropped it there, I take it, intending a scurrilous jest against your reverence.") The sexton also asks about the great red letter *A* in the sky, which he suggests symbolizes "Angel," in recognition of Governor Winthrop's death. Dimmesdale denies having heard about a mysterious *A* in the heavens.

Commentary

This chapter, the second of three crucial "scaffold chapters," appears exactly in the middle of the novel. Again, Hawthorne gathers all of his major characters in one place—this time in a chapter so foreboding, so convincing in its psychology and so rich in its symbolism that the chapter is unquestionably one of the most powerful in the novel.

In his description of Dimmesdale's actions while he is alone on the scaffold, Hawthorne demonstrates his mastery of psychological realism. The sudden changes in mood which take place in the minister's tired mind, the self-condemnation for his cowardice, the near-insanity of his scream, and his impulse to speak to Mr. Wilson all are developed convincingly.

Although one would hesitate to mention Freudian parallels, Hawthorne does suggest the subconscious expression of Dimmesdale's suppressed desires. For example, Dimmesdale's walking to the very spot where he should have stood seven years ago and acknowledged his sin takes place "perhaps actually under the influence of a species of somnambulism." Furthermore, Dimmesdale's shriek, which is heard by at least two people and which could have led to his being discovered on the scaffold, is released "without any effort of his will, or power to restrain himself." The impulse to speak to the Reverend Mr. Wilson is, again, an irrational urge from which "the minister could hardly restrain himself." So strong is the impulse, that Dimmesdale for an instant believes that he has actually spoken. His loud laugh, which announces his presence to Hester and Pearl, comes "unawares, and to his own infinite alarm." Finally, the "tumultuous rush of new life" which he feels when standing linked to Hester and Pearl appears to be his subconscious, urging him to acknowledge the link which joins all three of them.

Previously, we have seen Dimmesdale's conscious mind attempting to reason through the problem of his concealed guilt. In contrast, in this chapter, we see the tortured workings of his subconscious mind, which is the real source of his agony. When Dimmesdale is forced, by Pearl's repeated question, to bring the issue into the open, his fear of confession still dominates his subconscious desire to confess. His two refusals to publicly acknowledge his relationship with Hester and Pearl suggest Peter's first two denials of Christ.

Hawthorne's flair for Gothic detail is demonstrated in the appearance of a spectacular, weird light and the startling revelation of the diabolical Roger Chillingworth, who is standing near the scaffold. However, although both details have the effect of supernatural occurrences, Hawthorne is careful to give a natural explanation for each of them. The light, Hawthorne says, "was doubtless caused by one of those meteors, which the night-watcher may so often observe, burning out to waste."

Of course, however, the meteor seemed otherwise to those who saw it: "Nothing was more common, in those days, than to interpret all meteoric appearances . . . as so many revelations from a supernatural source." And the question of whether the ominous red *A* appeared at all is ambiguous. Although the sexton refers to the letter, Hawthorne suggests that the *A* may have appeared only in Dimmesdale's imagination: "We impute it . . . solely to the disease in his own eye and heart, that the minister, looking upward to the zenith, beheld there the appearance of an immense letter." Similarly, Chillingworth's appearance, although it suggests his knowledge of Dimmesdale's whereabouts, is logically explained by his having attended the dying Governor Winthrop.

This chapter abounds in symbols: the scaffold itself; Dimmesdale's standing on it; the three potential observers representing Church, State, and the World of Evil; the "electric chain" of Hester, Pearl, and Dimmesdale; Pearl's appeal to Dimmesdale; the revealing light from the heavens; and the variation on the letter *A*.

All in all, this is Hawthorne at his best and most typical.

13. ANOTHER VIEW OF HESTER

Summary

Hester is shocked at the change which she sees in Dimmesdale. While his intellect remains strong, his nerves are frayed and on edge. He seems to be a ruin of his former self. But the seven years since Pearl's birth have brought changes to Hester also. Her quiet, uncomplaining acceptance of her position and her untiring services to the sick, the poor, and the troubled have won her much respect among those townspeople who once condemned her. In fact, the public memory of her sin has dimmed, and the letter *A* which originally stood for "Adultery" is said by many to now stand for "Able." Some people even attribute to the embroidered letter a supernatural power to protect its wearer.

Hester has changed physically, as well. The warmth, charm, and passion which she once possessed appear to have been replaced by coldness, severity, and drabness. Her luxuriant hair is now hidden by a cap. She performs many services to the community, but she does so with the air of a lowly servant. Only in the care and education of Pearl does Hester demonstrate any of her earlier warmth and enthusiasm – and Pearl's abnormal nature baffles and saddens her. At times, Hester's mind is so troubled that she wonders whether it wouldn't be better if both she and Pearl were dead. The fact that Hester can contemplate suicide (an unpardonable sin in the Puritan faith) indicates that "the scarlet letter had not done its office."

In her recent awareness of Dimmesdale's painful misery, Hester has found a new object for her emotional energies. She realizes that Dimmesdale is on the verge of madness, and she feels that her promise to keep Chillingworth's identity a secret is largely responsible for Dimmesdale's illness. Hester decides to talk with Chillingworth at the first opportunity. One afternoon, walking on the peninsula with Pearl, Hester has that opportunity when she sees Chillingworth collecting herbs.

Commentary

Again, Hawthorne devotes a chapter to bringing us up to date on the development of one of his chief characters – in this case, Hester. And again, the information is provided entirely through summary and discussion, without one word of dialogue or one incident of dramatic action. Fortunately for the novel, these expository chapters are spaced so as not to kill the story's movement. Nonetheless, and despite the value of this chapter in developing a deeper understanding of Hester, many readers are likely to find these pages of summary rather tedious.

14. HESTER AND THE PHYSICIAN

Summary

Seeing Chillingworth, Hester sends Pearl to play in the shallow waters of the sea while she speaks to the old physician. Chillingworth greets her courteously, gives her compliments which he has heard concerning her behavior, and then he tells her that there is talk that she may be allowed to remove her scarlet letter. Hester denies the right of the magistrates to remove the letter, and she says, "Were I worthy to be quit of it, it would fall away of its own nature, or be transformed into something that should speak a different purport."

As she talks with Chillingworth, Hester is shocked at the change which has occurred in him over the past seven years. Chillingworth's fierce, dark face and the occasional red glare in his eyes testify to the evil purpose that has been dominating his life. He has been transformed into a devil.

Hester tells Chillingworth how she regrets having promised to keep his identity secret, thus enabling him to get his clutches on Dimmesdale. Chillingworth protests that, as Dimmesdale's physician, he should receive credit for keeping the minister alive. But when Hester suggests that Dimmesdale would have been better off dead, Chillingworth admits, with a kind of fierce pride, that he has tortured the minister. He describes what has taken place by saying, "A mortal man [Chillingworth], with once a human heart, has become a fiend for his [Dimmesdale's] especial torment!" And he suggests that, rather than having paid for his sin, Dimmesdale has increased it because he has made Chillingworth the fiend which he has become. Hester cries out that she is as guilty as Dimmesdale. She pleads for mercy, asking to be freed from her promise concerning the physician's identity.

At that moment, despite the wide chasm between them, Chillingworth and Hester share a feeling of mutual pity. The physician says that since the moment of the adultery, his torture of Dimmesdale has been "a dark necessity." Hester is not really sinful, nor is he, Chillingworth, fiend-like. It is fate which has created the tragic situation. As for telling Dimmesdale the secret of Chillingworth's identity, Chillingworth says that Hester may do as she wishes.

Commentary

Just as the preceding chapter showed us what had happened to Dimmesdale and Hester during the seven years since Pearl was born, this chapter fills us in on what has happened to Chillingworth. Here, however, Hawthorne manages to combine his character portrayal with a dramatic scene containing great pathos. Hester's misery as she senses her responsibility for Dimmesdale's suffering and for Chillingworth's moral deterioration evokes the physician's sympathy. Once again, Hawthorne saves Chillingworth from appearing merely as a symbol of evil personified. Instead, Hawthorne puts words in Chillingworth's mouth, rather than writing them as his own view, and thus, much can be made of the final speech, with its denial of freedom of the will.

The suggestion, however, that Chillingworth is powerless to resist the dictates of fate (a suggestion which was also made in Chapter 10) does not, in Hawthorne's view, excuse Chillingworth from responsibility for his own actions. But it does make it possible for the reader to sympathize with him, even while condemning him.

15. HESTER AND PEARL

Summary

Chillingworth leaves Hester and goes back to picking his herbs. He is an ugly and deformed old man whose gray beard nearly touches the ground when he stoops over. Hester looks at him and says bitterly, "Be it sin or no . . . I hate the man!" She feels that when Chillingworth married her, he committed a worse sin than any she ever committed against him.

During the conversation between the adults, Pearl has, with the aid of her imagination, been playing games along the seashore. She has made herself a scarf and cap of seaweed, and she has arranged eel-grass on her bosom in the shape of a green letter A.

Seeing Pearl dressed so symbolically, Hester tells her that the green letter on the child's bosom has no meaning. She asks Pearl if she knows what the scarlet A means. Pearl replies that Hester has to wear the scarlet letter for the same reason that the minister, Dimmesdale, keeps his hand over his heart.

At first amused, Hester quickly pales at the implication of the child's answer, but under further questioning, Pearl denies knowing the meaning of the letter. She asks her mother, three times: "What does the letter mean, mother?—and why dost thou wear it?—and why does the minister keep his hand over his heart?"

Hester is tempted to tell Pearl the truth in an effort to establish a bond of sympathy and understanding with the child, but she knows that she cannot answer the questions truthfully. Instead, Hester replies that she knows nothing about the minister's heart, and that she herself wears the letter A "for the sake of the gold-thread." But these answers do not satisfy Pearl, who keeps repeating her questions until the next morning. Finally, Hester threatens to shut Pearl in a dark closet unless the child quits teasing her.

Commentary

This chapter is divided into two sections. In the first section, Hawthorne introduces us to Hester's inner feelings concerning Chillingworth. Despite the moment of mutual pity which Hester shares with Chillingworth in the preceding chapter, here she feels a fierce hatred for him. She knows that by involving her in an unnatural, loveless marriage, Chillingworth set off the chain of events which led to her present suffering, and to Dimmesdale's suffering, as well. One should note, however, that although Hester is going beyond the letter of the law in accepting her punishment, she is not truly repentant at heart.

In the second half of the chapter, Hawthorne employs yet another variation on the symbolic letter A. He develops the character of Pearl as seen through Hester's eyes — emphasizing Pearl's wildness, touched occasionally with tenderness, her strong will and pride, and her sometimes remarkable ability to sense truths which most seven-year-olds are not capable of understanding.

The pathetic loneliness of Hester's position is vividly dramatic — especially as she wonders whether or not she should make Pearl a real friend and confide to her at least part of the truth about the letter A. Only two adults besides Hester know the full story, and it is neither convenient nor pleasant for Hester to discuss this matter with them.

Hester has no one to whom she can unburden her mind except to Pearl, this elf-like little girl who is Hester's companion twenty-four hours a day. It is natural that Hester is tempted to take Pearl into her confidence, and it is sad that, instead, Hester avoids satisfying her daughter's curiosity. In doing so, Hester finds it necessary to lie about the reason that she must wear the scarlet letter. As Hawthorne points out, this is the first time in seven years that Hester has been "false to the symbol on her bosom."

16. A FOREST WALK

Summary

Hester is anxious to tell Dimmesdale the true identity of Chillingworth, but she doesn't want to go to his apartment. For several days, she tries unsuccessfully to intercept him on one of his frequent walks along the shore or through the woods. Then, one day she hears that Dimmesdale is spending the night with the missionary John Eliot at a nearby Indian village and that he is expected back the following afternoon.

The next day, Hester goes with Pearl into the forest, hoping to meet Dimmesdale on his return home. As she and Pearl are walking along the chilly, narrow path through the dense woods, flickering gleams of sunshine break through the heavy gray clouds above them. Pearl suggests that the sunshine is running away from Hester because of the A on her bosom. In contrast, Pearl being a child without any such letter on her breast, runs and "catches" a patch of light. Symbolically, as Hester approaches and reaches toward the sunshine, it disappears.

Pearl then asks Hester to tell her about the Black Man. The child has overheard an old woman telling about this "man" who haunts the forest, getting people to sign their names with blood in his heavy iron-bound book, and then putting his mark on their bosoms. The old dame has said that the scarlet A is the Black Man's mark on Hester. Under Pearl's questioning, this time Hester confesses, "Once in my life I met the Black Man! . . . This scarlet letter is his mark!"

Having reached the depths of the forest, Hester and Pearl sit on a heap of moss beside a brook. As Pearl listens to the melancholy babble of the stream, she asks her mother why it is so sad. Hester replies that if Pearl had a sorrow like hers, she might understand the sad song of the brook. Just then, footsteps are heard on the path.

Hester sends Pearl away, but not before the girl has asked whether it is the Black Man approaching and whether Dimmesdale holds his hand over his heart to cover the Black Man's sign. As Pearl moves away along the brook, her singing mingles with the mournful sound of the stream.

The man coming up the path is Dimmesdale, looking haggard and feeble, and, with the aid of a staff, moving listlessly as though he has no purpose or desire to live. He holds his hand over his heart.

Commentary

This chapter and the four chapters which follow it contain the longest section of continuous dramatic action in the book. Although the novel covers seven years (even longer, if one counts the "Conclusion"), fully one-fifth of its total words are concentrated here, during the action of this single, crucial day. This particular chapter serves primarily to set the stage for the confession to follow, and, in addition, it is rich in atmosphere and symbolism. The chilly gloom of the forest almost perfectly reflects Hester's state of mind and the mood of the following scene. Nearly every element mentioned in the chapter carries some symbolic significance.

The narrow footpath through the dense forest is suggestive of the symbolic "narrow path" which Hester has been forced to follow for the past seven years. She sees the forest itself as the "moral wilderness in which she had so long been wandering." The obvious significance of the sunshine's fleeing from Hester and not allowing her to "catch it" is complicated by the irony of the ever-vivacious Pearl's appearing to easily "absorb" the sunshine. The story of the Black Man and his mark is described as a "common superstition," yet, for Hester (as her confession to Pearl implies), the Black Man and his mark have a special, personal meaning.

The brook is suggestive of Pearl, "inasmuch as the current of her life gushed from a well-spring as mysterious, and had flowed through scenes shadowed as heavily with gloom." In addition, the difference between the song of the brook and the song of the girl is also symbolically significant. Pearl, unlike the brook and unlike Hester, has never gone through a solemn experience, nor has she known sorrow which can lead to melancholy. The minister's hand over his heart (again linked with Hester's scarlet letter in this chapter) is yet another symbol, highlighted by Pearl's questions about its significance.

We also see Hester's concern over Dimmesdale and her bewilderment over the sprightly and inquisitive Pearl. And again, we see Pearl's uncanny genius for making comments and asking questions which suggest a knowledge which she doesn't possess. In the closing lines of the chapter, we see how far the physical and emotional deterioration of the pathetic Dimmesdale has progressed.

17. THE PASTOR AND HIS PARISHIONER

Summary

When Dimmesdale realizes that Hester is calling to him, he stops in surprise and looks anxiously toward the voice. He appears relieved to find that it is really Hester rather than a spirit calling him. Tense and silent, the two people go into the woods, where they sit on a bed of moss. At first, they are both ill at ease, and so they put off talking about what is really on their minds, as they attempt casual conversation about the weather and about each other's health.

Finally, Dimmesdale asks Hester, "Hast thou found peace?" Smiling drearily at her scarlet letter, she returns his question. Dimmesdale answers, "None! – nothing but despair!" He explains the misery of his ironic position: he is a minister who is idolized by his congregation, but he is carrying a dark sin concealed in his heart.

Hester gently suggests that his deep repentance and his good works have atoned for his sin, but Dimmesdale rejects her comfort and says, "Happy are you, Hester, that wear the scarlet letter openly upon your bosom! Mine burns in secret!" He adds that if there were anyone, friend or enemy, to whom he could speak openly of his sin, confession might save him. Hester replies that he has such a friend in her. Then, with great effort, she forces herself to go on: "Thou hast long had such an enemy, and dwellest with him, under the same roof!"

Dimmesdale leaps to his feet, clutches at his heart, and cries out in pain. Hester understands the awful nature of his situation, and she begs for Dimmesdale's forgiveness as she tells him that Chillingworth is her husband.

Dimmesdale frowns fiercely at her, then sinks to the ground, saying that he cannot forgive her for letting Chillingworth victimize him. As she pleads with Dimmesdale, though, he eventually does forgive her. Then Dimmesdale declares that Chillingworth's sin is greater than either Hester's or his own, for Chillingworth "violated the sanctity of a human heart." But Dimmesdale hushes Hester when she suggests that what they did "had a consecration [a sacredness] of its own."

As the two sit holding hands, reluctant to leave the peace of the forest, Dimmesdale's terror at the thought of Chillingworth grows until he sees death as his only escape. He appeals to Hester to think for him and be his strength.

Hester accepts the challenge, even though she weeps to see him so weak. She urges him to leave Boston and start a new life elsewhere. Dimmesdale resists, so she makes a stronger statement, telling him to change his name and take up a new life: "Preach! Write! Act! Do anything save to lie down and die!" Dimmesdale is momentarily excited by her suggestion, even though he knows that he lacks the strength to start a new life alone. To this, Hester answers, in a deep whisper, "Thou shalt not go alone!"

Commentary

In earlier scenes, Hawthorne put his characters together in almost every possible combination – except for that of Hester and Dimmesdale. These two people have appeared together only seldom and briefly, and never alone. There has been no intimate conversation between the two, and the reader, while realizing that Hester and Dimmesdale are fellow sinners, has probably not – until now – really conceived of them as being passionate lovers.

This chapter, then, is a key chapter in the development of the love story which is a central part of this novel. After seven long years of being apart, unable to discuss matters freely with each other, now they are about to talk about the secret which they share between them. At last they are alone to talk about the consequence of their love affair.

Their tension at the opening of the chapter is easily understood. It is also clear that Hester retains a spark of her former passion for Dimmesdale. Remember that she arranged this conversation for one purpose: to save Dimmesdale from Chillingworth.

The spark of passion between the two grows warmer as Hester sees the intensity of Dimmesdale's suffering. She cries out for his forgiveness, and she recalls tenderly their "consecrated" love affair. And then finally, and of key importance, Hester realizes that Dimmesdale, with all his weaknesses, needs her and her strength.

Although Hester's present emotions may seem more like pity than like the passion which she once felt for Dimmesdale years ago, it is strong enough that she is prepared to leave Boston and take up a new life with Dimmesdale, wherever he may go.

Hawthorne also gives us a new view of Dimmesdale. Dimmesdale's weakness and his sense of guilt, which have long been apparent, are shown even more strongly as he unburdens his heart to Hester. But whereas previously we have seen Dimmesdale as only a minister whose outward behavior is so proper as to make us wonder how he ever could have passionately committed the sin of adultery, here we get a glimpse of him as a man whose passions are not always under perfect control.

Dimmesdale's cry of anguished despair at hearing about Chillingworth, his fierce frown and his enraged accusation of Hester, his appeal for her help, and his stressing the word "alone" as a kind of implied proposal, all tend to humanize him and make him a more believable lover. And if it is true that opposites attract, then certainly Dimmesdale, too weak to take a step alone, and Hester, with strength enough for both of them, should be mutually attractive to each other.

The suggestion of Dimmesdale's own scarlet *A* is reinforced in this chapter when he refers to the letter which Hester wears openly. Note that Dimmesdale says, "Mine burns in secret!"

18. A FLOOD OF SUNSHINE

Summary

Hester was born in England, and she has a strong, independent mind and strong passions. She was never a Puritan, and for seven years, she has not even been a "proper" member of Boston's Puritan society. Thus, her decision to leave Boston is not difficult. After all, Boston has never been "home" for her.

For Dimmesdale, however, the decision to leave Boston is terribly difficult. He is a Puritan minister. His entire life (except for his one sinful act of passion with Hester) has been strictly governed by the Puritan code. He will be leaving behind everything that has been of great value to him.

But it is Hester's strength and assurance that finally convince him that – if she accompanies him – he can, and should, start a new life. Thus, Dimmesdale agrees to leave Boston.

He immediately feels a sudden surge of joy. Hester also feels exhilarated by their decision to leave Boston. She removes the scarlet letter and throws it on the bank of the brook. Then, removing her cap, she lets her rich, dark hair fall about her shoulders. Her youth, her beauty, and her femininity suddenly return to her as she stands there, radiant and alive. Appropriately, the sun breaks through, and the forest – which had once been so gloomy – becomes bright and cheerful.

In the excitement of their new relationship, Hester remembers that Dimmesdale hardly knows their daughter. When she mentions this fact, Dimmesdale says that he is afraid that Pearl may not like him. Hester, however, is so joyously anticipating their living together as a family that she is absolutely sure that having a father will bring happiness and a sense of well-being to her bewildering little girl.

Hester calls to Pearl, who has been playing in the forest. The child, who seems so wild in the village, appears to be in her true element here. The forest, as though recognizing Pearl's intrinsic nature, accepts her as one of its own. The animals do not run from her, and the wildflowers seem pleased when she gathers them to decorate her hair and dress. Hearing her mother's call, she leaves her playing and comes slowly toward the two adults.

Commentary

Here in the forest, where nature's principles – rather than the laws of man – operate, Hester and Dimmesdale have yielded to natural impulses, and, here in this natural setting, Nature has symbolically indicated her approval by flooding the scene in a sudden burst of sunshine.

Mistakenly thinking that he can change what has happened in the past, Dimmesdale becomes exuberant at the thought of escaping with Hester. Similarly, Hester is also exuberant. She throws off her scarlet *A*, the symbol of her shame, and she lets down her beautiful, glossy hair. Once again, she stands proud and vibrant.

In this scene, Hawthorne has written one of the most vivid and sensuous passages in the novel. The obvious symbolism of the forest's accepting Pearl reminds the reader again that Pearl was born of a natural union, rather than from a socially sanctioned Puritan union. With all three of the family group now molding their behavior to the laws of nature, rather than to the laws of man, it appears as though Dimmesdale, Hester, and Pearl may be able, at last, to find some happiness in life. But there are discouraging omens – especially Dimmesdale's repeated fears that Pearl will not accept him, and the slowness with which Pearl approaches her parents.

19. THE CHILD AT THE BROOK-SIDE

Summary

As Pearl approaches her mother and father, her natural beauty is clearly enhanced by the flowers that she is wearing. In fact, Hester comments on Pearl's sudden resemblance to her father, and Dimmesdale confesses that he has often feared that the resemblance might be apparent to others.

Pearl stops on the other side of the brook, despite her mother's encouragement to come and meet "a friend of mine, who must be thy friend also." Subconsciously, Dimmesdale covers his heart with his hand. Pearl points toward her mother's breast and frowns as Hester continues to try to coax her across the brook. As Hester's requests turn to commands, Pearl, still pointing toward her mother's bosom, bursts into a passionate, shrieking fit of rage. At last, Hester realizes that the missing scarlet letter is responsible for Pearl's strange behavior.

Dimmesdale says that Hester must do whatever is necessary to calm the child, and so, sadly, Hester tells Pearl to bring her the scarlet *A* from the bank of the stream. When Pearl refuses, Hester retrives the *A*, pins it on her bosom, and tucks her hair once again under her cap. Instantly, her warmth and femininity disappear and her face gives off the look of dreary resignation that Pearl is used to. The child now bounds across the brook, kisses her mother, and then appears to mock her by kissing the scarlet letter also.

Hester asks Pearl to go to the minister, explaining that he loves them both. But Pearl resists, asking, "Will he go back with us, hand in hand, we three together, into the town?" Hester answers that Dimmesdale won't go with them now, but that in the future, they will all live together and love each other.

At this, Pearl asks whether Dimmesdale will always keep his hand over his heart. Hester replies, "Foolish child, what a question is that! . . . Come and ask his blessing!" And only by force does Hester bring the reluctant Pearl to the minister. Trying to win Pearl's friendship, Dimmesdale kisses her, but the child runs to the brook and washes his kiss away, then stands alone as Hester and Dimmesdale make final plans for their escape from Boston. The melancholy brook has another tale now to add to its cheerless, mysterious babble.

Commentary

While reading through this chapter, one should recall the passage (in Chapter 2) in which Hester was tempted to hold Pearl up so as to cover the scarlet letter *A* on her bosom. At that time, Hester realized that "one token of her shame would but poorly serve to hide another." Here, Pearl (the living symbol of Hester's sin) actually forces her mother to wear the scarlet letter after she tossed it away.

On the surface, Hawthorne may appear to be unrealistic in making a seven-year-old girl be such an obvious agent of Hester's punishment, but one should note Hester's logical explanation: "Children will not abide any, the slightest, change in the accustomed aspect of things that are daily before their eyes." One need not assume that Pearl recognizes the full significance of her demands; yet, the import of what Pearl insists that her mother do – fasten on the scarlet A once again – is apparent to Hester and to the reader.

There is also strong symbolic significance in Pearl's behavior toward Dimmesdale. Although Pearl kisses her mother after Hester has again donned the letter which acknowledges her sin, Pearl washes away Dimmesdale's kiss. It is also significant that Pearl's father has still not displayed any sign of his part in the affair (unlike Hester, who wears the scarlet A), and he still refuses to acknowledge Hester and Pearl in public.

Hawthorne does an excellent job of conveying his characters' emotions in this scene, especially in his description of Hester putting on her scarlet letter again. Her sadness at having to trade the sunshine of her new womanhood for the shadow of her past seven years is deepened by the fact that Dimmesdale, the man for whom she momentarily discarded the letter, asks her – for his own peace of mind – to put the symbol of their sin back on her bosom.

20. THE MINISTER IN A MAZE

Summary

Leaving the forest before Hester and Pearl, Dimmesdale begins thinking about their plans to escape to Europe. Hester is going to secretly book passage for two adults and a child on a Bristol-bound ship, due to leave Boston four days later, the day after Dimmesdale is scheduled to preach the important Election Day sermon. Excited by his decision to leave and begin a new life, the minister hurries along the forest path, showing none of his recent faint-heartedness and feebleness. As he comes into town, everything – especially his own church – appears somehow changed and unfamiliar.

The "change," however, is in the minister, not in the town, as is shown by his behavior toward the people whom he meets. Stopping to talk with an old respected deacon of his church, Dimmesdale can hardly resist uttering some blasphemy about the communion supper. He then meets a pious and devoted old widow whom he has often comforted with scriptural passages; today, however, he is unable to think of anything to say to her except an argument against the eternal life of the soul. As a compromise, he mutters confusedly and goes on.

Next, seeing a young virgin from his congregation, he is tempted to corrupt her with a look and a word. Instead, though, he hurries by her—but he is not yet free from torment. He is swept by other irrational urges—to teach wicked words to some Puritan children and to exchange handshakes and oaths with a drunken Spanish sailor. While Dimmesdale is puzzling over these wicked impulses, he meets Mistress Hibbins, who has a reputation of being a witch. She greets him familiarly, refers to his visit to the forest, laughs knowingly at his denial of any evil doing, and she promises to meet him at midnight in the forest.

Wondering whether he has really sold his soul to the devil, Dimmesdale arrives at his apartment. That familiar place, where two days before he was writing his Election Day sermon, also looks strange to him. Then he realizes that the change is not in the apartment; it is within himself.

Chillingworth enters, inquires about Dimmesdale's trip to the Indian camp, about Dimmesdale's health, and then he recommends some medicine to strengthen the minister in preparation for the day of his important sermon. Dimmesdale declines Chillingworth's medicine, and, suspecting that Chillingworth may know something about the secret plan to sail from Boston, he says that he may not be with his congregation for another year. Chillingworth leaves then, and Dimmesdale burns what he has written as a sermon and sits up all night, writing a new Election Day sermon.

Commentary

By showing us the change in Dimmesdale, especially in his series of temptations toward some wild and wicked actions, Hawthorne shows us the deep, subconscious effects of Dimmesdale's natural inclination toward the romantic, the emotional, and the irrational. Until his talk with Hester, Dimmesdale's strong, rational Puritan conscience struggled successfully with his emotions. Now, however, Dimmesdale "yielded himself, with deliberate choice, as he had never done before, to what he knew was deadly sin." This chapter should be compared with Chapter 12, in which Dimmesdale's subconscious tries to make his guilt known. It is chapters like these that reveal the depths of Hawthorne's psychological insight into the human heart.

21. THE NEW ENGLAND HOLIDAY

Summary

On Election Day, one of the most important Puritan holidays, Hester and Pearl start out for the crowded marketplace. Hester appears as drab and quiet as ever, but inside, she burns with the knowledge that she will soon leave Boston, and the life of the scarlet letter, and will once again resume her role as a woman. Pearl, who is especially dressed in bright, vivid colors today, is livelier than ever – as though she is demonstrating the excitement which Hester feels but cannot show.

As Hester and Pearl reach the bustling marketplace, Pearl becomes even more excited and asks her mother about the crowd of people dressed in their Sunday clothes. After Hester explains to her about the procession of prominent men who will soon be passing, Pearl asks whether Reverend Dimmesdale will be in the procession and whether he will hold out his hands to them.

When she is told that Dimmesdale will be there, but that they must not greet him, Pearl comments on Dimmesdale's strange behavior. She is very aware that he feels free to recognize them at night and in the woods, but that he refuses to recognize them in the daylight or among people: "A strange, sad man is he, with his hand always over his heart."

Meanwhile, the motley crowd (which is made up of restrained, stiff Puritans, a colorful party of Indians, and several rough-looking sailors) is growing larger. Chillingworth arrives, accompanied by the picturesque commander of the Bristol-bound ship. The commander leaves Chillingworth and stops to talk with Hester, who is standing somewhat apart from the crowd. She is startled when the commander jovially refers to an extra passenger who has just booked passage – the old physician, Chillingworth! He explains to Hester that Chillingworth has described himself as being a friend of both Hester and "the gentleman that you spoke of." From across the public square, Hester sees Chillingworth smiling at her.

Commentary

Although some readers may find Hawthorne's discussion of the Election Day celebration somewhat of an unwelcome intrusion, the description is interesting evidence both of Hawthorne's historical knowledge and of his attitude toward the early American Puritan society. Note, too, that there is pointed satire in Hawthorne's comment that on this most festive day, the people "compressed whatever mirth and public joy they deemed allowable to human infirmity; thereby so far dispelling the customary cloud, that, for the space of a single holiday, they appeared scarcely more grave than most other communities at a period of general affliction."

Hawthorne then softens his judgment somewhat, as he goes on to account for their severe-seeming mood. He points out the contrast between the Puritans' somber clothes and the colorful attire of the Indians and the sailors. This, of course, is another reminder that the Puritans were forbidden to act as freely as the sailors. The era was definitely a time when people were deadly serious about religion and day-to-day living and about public, as well as private, behavior. This day, however, was one of the very few days that they allowed themselves to show a little joy. It is a special day, and it is the day that will mark the climax of the novel.

Pearl's comments regarding Dimmesdale's behavior remind the reader, once more, what action the minister must take if he is to bring peace to his tortured conscience. Note too the subtlety and determination shown in Chillingworth's having arranged to keep Dimmesdale in his clutches. Clearly, Dimmesdale's escape will not be an easy one.

It is important to note that although Hester learns that her and Dimmesdale's plans to escape have been discovered, there is no indication that Dimmesdale knows about Chillingworth's plans to board the ship that will carry Hester, Dimmesdale, and Pearl away. Hester has no opportunity to tell Dimmesdale between the time she learns it and the time that Dimmesdale emerges from the church (Chapter 23).

22. THE PROCESSION

Summary

Before Hester can recover from the shock of hearing the ship captain tell her that Chillingworth has also booked passage, the Election Day procession begins. First comes the military band, not good, but stirring; then the local troops, brilliant in their plumes and their burnished steel armor; next, the civil authorities, impressively distinguished; and following them, the Reverend Mr. Dimmesdale. With his head high and his step firm, Dimmesdale shows none of the depression or physical weakness which has characterized him for some time.

Seeing Dimmesdale pass by, Hester is disappointed and depressed when he doesn't give her even a brief glance. The change in Dimmesdale (since their talk three days ago in the forest) is so great that Pearl does not even recognize her father as he passes. In fact, she says that had she recognized him, she would have run to him and asked him to kiss her before all these people. "What would the minister have said, mother? Would he have clapped his hand over his heart, and scowled on me, and bid me be gone?" Hester quickly silences Pearl, reprimanding her for her foolishness.

Mistress Hibbins, feared and avoided by the people of Boston, joins Hester. She refers to "the meeting" in the forest and suggests that Dimmesdale, the "saint on earth" who just passed, carries on his breast the mark of the Black Man. That mark, Mistress Hibbins says, will be disclosed to the world. Then she departs, laughing shrilly.

The service has already begun in the meeting house, and from her position by the scaffold, Hester can hear the rich, musical voice of Dimmesdale as he delivers the Election Day sermon. Although she cannot distinguish the words, she detects the sorrow and anguish of a human heart revealing a secret and beseeching sympathy and forgiveness.

Meanwhile, Pearl is amusing herself by playing in the marketplace, looking at the wild Indians and the rough, swarthy seamen. She is such a striking contrast to the somber Puritans that the ship's captain tries to catch her and give her a kiss. Unable to capture the lively creature, he throws her the gold chain from his hat. As Pearl twines it around her body, the captain asks her to take her mother a message: Tell her, he says, that the hump-shouldered old doctor will bring "his friend" aboard the ship, and that Hester need not concern herself further.

Hester's spirits sink as Pearl relays the captain's words. She is depressed by the news and by the growing circle of people — Indians, sailors, and townspeople — who suddenly surround her, staring rudely and inquisitively at her scarlet mark of sin. Ironically, at the same moment, another group of townspeople is looking up to Dimmesdale in his pulpit as if he were a saint. "What imagination would have been irreverent enough to surmise that the same scorching stigma was on them both!"

Commentary

Hawthorne continues to prepare the ground for the climax which is to follow. Dimmesdale is the focus of attention in this chapter as surely as he is the focus of attention in the Election Day procession. But his apparent strength is only temporary. His physical appearance contrasts sharply with his physical appearance in the past, but even more strikingly with the Dimmesdale we are to see in the following chapter.

The strings of dramatic tension are all drawn tightly here, as Hawthorne brings in each of the major characters and their relationship with Dimmesdale. Hester's warm recollection of Dimmesdale's tenderness in the forest and her disappointment when he ignores her on Election Day remind us of the impossibility of Hester and Dimmesdale's ever finding happiness in Puritan New England—as long as Dimmesdale's position as a pure, spotless man of God is a fraud. Pearl's desire for Dimmesdale's recognition and her reference to his hand over his heart, once more repeated, emphasizes again the primary obstacle in their relationship. And the ship captain's news that Chillingworth, rather than Hester, is now in charge of the minister shows that Dimmesdale is almost powerless.

The point of crisis has arrived, and the problem is entirely Dimmesdale's. He alone has the chance and the responsibility to take the decisive act. The seven long years of contrast between the fellow-sinners—Hester and Dimmesdale—are especially apparent here. Within Puritan society, Hester and Dimmesdale will always stand on opposite sides of a vast gulf, as long as Dimmesdale maintains his fraudulent pose as a man of purity and holiness. What Dimmesdale must do if he is ever to find peace is to cross that gulf and acknowledge Hester, stand by her side, and hold Pearl's hand in his, announcing to the public that he and Hester love one another and that Pearl is their child.

23. THE REVELATION OF THE SCARLET LETTER

Summary

At the end of Dimmesdale's Election Day sermon, the crowd emerges from the church; they are extremely enthusiastic about the inspired and powerful words which they have just heard from a man whom they feel is soon to die. Seemingly, this is the most brilliant and triumphant moment in Dimmesdale's public life.

As the procession of dignitaries which has formed to march to a banquet at the town hall approaches the marketplace, the feelings of the crowd are expressed in a spontaneous shout of tribute. "Never, on New England soil, has stood the man so honored by his mortal brethren, as the preacher!" They are speaking, of course, about Dimmesdale.

But the shout dies to a murmur as the people see Dimmesdale tottering feebly and nervously in the procession. His face has taken on a deathly pallor, and he can scarcely walk. The Reverend Mr. Wilson attempts to give some support to Dimmesdale, but the minister repels him and struggles on until he comes to the scaffold, where Hester stands holding Pearl by the hand. There, Dimmesdale pauses. Governor Bellingham leaves his place in the procession to help Dimmesdale, but he is strangely repelled by a certain "something" in the minister's appearance.

As Dimmesdale turns to the scaffold, he calls Hester and Pearl to his side. Suddenly, Chillingworth appears and attempts to stop Dimmesdale, but Dimmesdale scorns the old physician and cries out to Hester to help him get up to the scaffold. The crowd watches in astonishment as the minister, leaning on Hester and holding Pearl's hand, ascends the scaffold steps. Chillingworth's face darkens as he realizes that nowhere else but on the scaffold can Dimmesdale escape him.

Dimmesdale tells Hester that he is dying and must acknowledge his shame. Then he turns to the crowd and cries out his guilt. He steps in front of Hester and Pearl and declares that on his breast he bears the sign of his sin. He tears the ministerial band from his breast and, for a moment, he stands flushed with triumph before the horrified crowd. Then he sinks down upon the scaffold.

Hester lifts Dimmesdale's head and cradles it against her bosom. Chillingworth, meanwhile, kneels down and, in a tone of defeat, keeps repeating, "Thou hast escaped me!" Dimmesdale asks God's forgiveness for Chillingworth's sin, then he turns to Pearl and, smiling sweetly, he asks for a kiss. Pearl kisses him and weeps.

Dimmesdale, obviously dying now, tells Hester farewell. She lowers her face to his and asks whether they will spend eternity together. Dimmesdale recalls their sin and says that he fears that eternal happiness is not to be hoped for. He leaves the matter to God, whose mercy he has seen in the afflictions leading to his public confession. His dying words are "Praised be his name! His will be done! Farewell!"

The crowd of Puritans, which has been silent, suddenly breaks out in a "strange, deep voice of awe and wonder."

Commentary

This chapter contains the third and final scaffold scene, and it brings the novel to its dramatic climax and its solution. Dimmesdale's decisive act – to climb upon the scaffold, join hands with Hester and Pearl, and publicly confess his sin of adultery – is his greatest personal triumph. In addition, his confession enables him to escape from Chillingworth's sadistic clutches.

What Hawthorne makes most clear in this chapter is the fact that Dimmesdale must do this final act alone. Symbolically, Dimmesdale rejects the help of Reverend Wilson (a representative of the church) and of Governor Bellingham (a representative of the state). He turns only to Hester for some support in his moment of crisis, and even she cannot help him beyond a certain point. She cannot take the necessary step for him. Dimmesdale alone must step forward to expose his breast. Afterward, Dimmesdale is drained of his strength, and he collapses. Once again, it is Hester on whom he leans. But, once again, even she cannot assure him that his public act of repentance is better than their plan to escape from Boston. Hawthorne has clearly made the minister the key actor in the climax of the novel.

Dimmesdale's recognition of his daughter takes place in the form of a highly symbolic kiss. Earlier, you should note, Pearl washed away her father's kiss because "he was not true." Now she kisses him. This kiss not only symbolizes Pearl's acceptance and forgiveness of Dimmesdale, but it is proof that Pearl is changing – from being a cold, unreal, imp-like creature, she now becomes a human being, one who weeps human tears for the first time in the novel. Until now, Pearl has been almost entirely symbolic, a device of punishment; here, she becomes a person. "A spell was broken," Hawthorne tells us.

Thus, there is a solution, but very little joy, in the climax of this novel. Dimmesdale has won a long-delayed victory over himself, but he shows little elation or optimism. He has made his peace with God, but unlike Hester, who could have found happiness in their escape from Boston, Dimmesdale is too much the Puritan, too much a part of the Puritan community, to even be optimistic about the afterlife. He leaves his fate to God's will. Once, years ago, Dimmesdale willfully asserted his own passion, and the result was a lifetime of unhappiness and misery. He has learned not to will happiness for himself. He leaves that, in true Puritan tradition, to God.

24. CONCLUSION

The novel, in essence, ends with the preceding chapter. But like many writers of his time, Hawthorne addresses the reader here in order to explain and moralize about his story. Some modern readers are annoyed by this technique, but such a practice was quite common among novelists in the nineteenth century. Actually, this technique works extremely well here because the characters in this novel are so closely identified with Hawthorne's concepts and ideas.

For example, in the opening of the chapter, Hawthorne tells us that Dimmesdale's dramatic exposing of his own scarlet letter was variously reported and interpreted by those who witnessed the final scaffold scene. Some people contended that the minister had physically inflicted the mark on himself over several years as a kind of self-torture. Other people said that the mark was produced by Chillingworth's magic drugs. Still other people said that the symbol was produced from within, by the suffering of his spirit. Hawthorne leaves the interpretation optional by saying, "The reader may choose among these theories."

But Hawthorne complicates such a choice by adding that there were some witnesses who declared that there was no mark at all on Dimmesdale's breast and, furthermore, that the minister said nothing to link himself with Hester's sin. Here, however, Hawthorne suggests that "we must be allowed to consider this version of Mr. Dimmesdale's story as only an instance of that stubborn fidelity with which a man's friends – and especially a clergyman's – will sometimes uphold his character, when proofs, clear as the mid-day sunshine on the scarlet letter, establish him as a false and sin-stained creature of the dust."

To bring Dimmesdale's story to a conclusion, Hawthorne points to the central moral in specific terms: "Be true! Be true! Be true! Show freely to the world, if not your worst, yet some trait whereby the worst may be inferred!"

Concerning what happened to Chillingworth, Hawthorne tells us that because all of the doctor's energy was directed at revenge, Chillingworth had nothing to sustain him after Dimmesdale died. Hawthorne says that Chillingworth "shrivelled" and, within a year, he too was dead. Yet despite the fact that the doctor had become a fiend, Hawthorne offers a philosophical explanation of his actions which may lead to our viewing Chillingworth with mercy, if not approval.

Hatred and love, Hawthorne says, are so close as to seem, philosophically, to be "essentially the same." Hawthorne suggests that in the spiritual world "the physician and the minister – mutual victims as they have been – may, unawares, have found their earthly stock of hatred and antipathy transmuted into golden love." Although he finds Chillingworth's sin the most grievous in the book, Hawthorne is not Puritan enough to view the man coldly and vindictively.

Concerning what happened to Pearl, the "elf-child" who becomes human in the final scaffold scene, Hawthorne provides a "happy ending" which may strike the critical reader as rather trite and artificial. Having inherited a great deal of property from Chillingworth, Pearl becomes the "richest heiress of her day, in the New World." She might have married the "devoutest Puritan of them all" had she stayed in the colonies, but shortly after Dimmesdale's death, Hester takes Pearl to Europe. Hawthorne tells us that "none knew . . . whether the elf-child had gone thus untimely into a maiden grave, or whether her wild, rich nature had been softened and subdued, and made capable of a woman's gentle happiness." Hawthorne, however, gives strong hints that Pearl lived on in happiness and wealth, married well, had a child, and remained an affectionate and dutiful daughter to Hester. Hawthorne's kind treatment of Pearl may be largely caused by his desire to throw some ray of sunshine into a novel which he knew was extremely gloomy. But one must remember that whereas the other three characters were all involved in the tragedy of the scarlet letter because of their own individual sins, Pearl is a helpless victim.

Hawthorne's primary focus at the end of his novel is (as it was in the opening scenes) on Hester. We are told that although she stayed abroad for several years, she returned to her little cottage, which had been unoccupied since her departure. "Here had been her sin; here, her sorrow; and here was yet to be her penitence." Although the woman of the scarlet letter had already become a legend, and not even the sternest Puritan would have forced Hester to wear the scarlet *A* again, she put it on voluntarily and wore it the rest of her life.

Hawthorne makes it clear that Hester gained a kind of wisdom through her suffering. The people of the village viewed her with sorrow, awe, and reverence, and they – especially the women – came to her for guidance with their sorrows and problems. But Hester was not, even in this period of personal nobility, a Puritan. She was, rather, a defeated but still hopeful prophetess of a brighter period when the relentless Puritan morality would be replaced by a new moral order: "in Heaven's own time a new truth would be revealed, in order to establish the whole relation between man and woman on a surer ground of mutual happiness."

Hester continued to retain her faith that, someday, a woman "lofty, pure, and beautiful" would appear as the angel and apostle of revelation. "So said Hester Prynne, and glanced her sad eyes downward at the scarlet letter." Clearly, there is more of a touch of the Puritan in Hawthorne, though. He criticizes the severity of his Puritan ancestors in this novel, it is true, but he also requires Hester to pay a heavy price for having yielded once – and only once – to her passions.

After many years, Hester dies and is buried in that cemetery which Hawthorne described in the opening chapter. Her grave is "near that old and sunken grave" (Dimmesdale's) but "with a space between as if the dust of the two sleepers had no right to mingle." This statement recalls Dimmesdale's pessimistic words in the foregoing chapter: "It may be . . . vain to hope that we could meet hereafter, in an everlasting and pure reunion."

Hawthorne's final touch of symbolism lies in the slate tombstone which serves for both graves. Hawthorne uses the language of heraldry to describe the letter *A*, which is engraved on it and which "might serve for a motto and a brief description of our now concluded legend." He describes the tombstone as being somber and brightened only by one ever-glowing point of light, the scarlet letter *A*. A herald's description of the tombstone might read: "On a Field, Sable, the Letter *A*, Gules," which is translated into modern English as, "On a black background, the scarlet letter *A*."

CHARACTER ANALYSES

Hester Prynne

Hester is introduced as being young, tall, and beautiful, with an elegant figure, abundant glossy dark hair, a rich complexion, and deep-set black eyes.

She comes from an impoverished but genteel English family, having lived in a "decayed house of gray stone, with a poverty-stricken aspect, but retaining a half-obliterated shield of arms over the portal, in token of antique gentility." But even without that specific indication of her high birth, the reader would know that Hester is a lady, from her bearing and pride, especially in Chapter 2, when she bravely faces the humiliation of the scaffold: "And never had Hester Prynne appeared more lady-like, in the antique interpretation of the term, than as she issued from the prison."

It is Hester's pride which sustains her, from that opening scene until she dies, still wearing the scarlet *A*. And coupled with that pride is a passion which is demonstrated not only through her relations with Dimmesdale but also in her emotional attachment to Pearl, in her defiance of Governor Bellingham (Chapter 8), and even in her conversations with her husband, old Chillingworth (Chapters 4 and 14).

Hester's sin (committed about a year before the novel begins) is the sin which gives the book its title and around which the action of the book revolves. Adultery, prohibited by the Seventh Commandment, was so seriously condemned by the Puritans of seventeenth-century Massachusetts that it was often punished by death.

In contrast, Hawthorne does *not* condone Hester's adultery, but he does find it less serious a sin than the sins of Dimmesdale and Chillingworth. Clearly, Hawthorne sees Hester as a victim. He emphasizes, for example, that Hester is a victim of her own youth, living in an age which forced her to marry Chillingworth without loving him. Second, Hester is a victim of Chillingworth's selfishness, which permitted him to marry the young and passionate girl – knowing all the while that she did not return his love, and knowing that he was not suited to the role of her husband. Third, Hester is the victim of Chillingworth's stupidity in sending his young wife ahead of him to the Massachusetts colony while he remained in Amsterdam. Fourth, Hester is a victim of Fate, which led to Chillingworth's capture by the Indians, and left Hester without any word from him to indicate even that he was alive. And fifth, Hester is a victim of Dimmesdale's weakness; he allowed their love affair to develop when he knew that he was unprepared to either marry Hester or share responsibility for their child if she were to become pregnant—which she did, of course.

But the most important facts to note about Hester's sin of adultery are, first, that her sin was a sin of passion—rather than a sin of intellect. This fact distinguishes her from Chillingworth. He deliberately, with his intellect, sets out to destroy Dimmesdale. In addition, Hester's sin is openly acknowledged, rather than concealed in her heart. This fact distinguishes her from Dimmesdale, who chooses to hide his sin.

Hester did not, with deliberate calculation, plan to commit the sin of adultery, nor did she deliberately plan to do injury to others. That she deeply loved Dimmesdale is obvious throughout the book. Her fault was that her passion and her love were stronger than her respect for the New World's Puritan code of morals. As she says in Chapter 17, "What we did had a consecration of its own. We felt it so! We said so to each other!"

Although Hester is clearly not a Puritan, and it is doubtful that her respect for the Puritan code ever truly overcomes her independent passions, Hester does fully acknowledge her sin—and she boldly displays it to the world. The elaborateness with which she embroiders her symbol of shame, dresses Pearl in scarlet as a second symbol, and wears the scarlet *A* long after she could have removed it—all these facts are proof that she is trying to hide nothing. Hester's salvation lies in Truth.

When apologizing for having concealed Chillingworth's identity, she tells Dimmesdale (Chapter 17): "In all things else, I have striven to be true! Truth was the one virtue which I might have held fast, and did hold fast, through all extremity. . . . A lie is never good, even though death threaten on the other side!"

Hester learns from her sin, and she grows strong as a result of accepting her punishment. "The scarlet letter was her passport into regions where other women dared not tread. Shame, Despair, Solitude!

These had been her teachers – stern and wild ones – and they had made her strong." At the end of the novel, Hester emerges from her experiences and is revealed to be a woman capable of helping others and respected by them. She has the happiness that comes of being at peace with oneself, one's fellow men, and with one's God.

Arthur Dimmesdale

Dimmesdale is young, pale, and physically delicate. He has large, melancholy eyes and a tremulous mouth, suggesting great sensitivity. He also has that fresh and childlike quality which undoubtedly brings out the "mother instinct" in his female parishioners.

As an ordained minister, he is well educated, and he has a philosophical turn of mind. Yet, Dimmesdale is modest, and the eloquence of his sermons is of a quiet kind. There is no doubt that he is a devoted servant of God – passionate in his religion and effective in the pulpit – but, privately, he suffers from a tragic flaw. His flaw is his inability to publicly acknowledge that he committed adultery with Hester Prynne and is the father of her little girl, Pearl.

Adultery, however, is not Dimmesdale's worst sin. And, if Dimmesdale had had the courage to acknowledge his sin, then it would have been no more serious than Hester's. But Dimmesdale cannot acknowledge his adultery, and so an even worse sin than adultery is Dimmesdale's "concealed sin."

This "concealed sin" rankles in Dimmesdale's heart and is the cause of his terrible torment of conscience. Dimmesdale's concealed sin makes him, however, one of Hawthorne's most interesting psychological studies, and his case is made all the more interesting (and, of course, more painful) through the irony of Dimmesdale's being a minister, who is supposed to be absolutely pure, and who fervently urges his congregation to confess and openly repent of their sins. And, all the while, Dimmesdale knows that he himself is incapable of doing just that – confessing his own sin of adultery and repenting.

Why does Dimmesdale conceal his sin during seven long years of torment – both by Chillingworth and by his own conscience? In Chapter 10, Dimmesdale himself offers two possible explanations. Speaking in general terms about persons guilty of concealed sin, but obviously thinking of his own case, he says: "It may be that they are kept silent by the very constitution of their nature. Or – can we not suppose it – guilty as they may be, retaining, nevertheless, a zeal for

God's glory and man's welfare, they shrink from displaying themselves black and filthy in the view of men; because, thenceforward, no good can be achieved by them; no evil of the past be redeemed by better service."

The second reason that Dimmesdale offers for concealing his sin is this: he remains silent so that he can continue to do God's work as a minister. At first glance, this argument seems to have some logical appeal. Certainly Dimmesdale is a devoted and effective servant of God. He increasingly inspires his congregation during the seven years that we observe him. Certainly also, had Dimmesdale revealed his sin at the beginning of the novel, the church would have lost a good minister. Clearly, however, Dimmesdale is rationalizing, or trying to justify his behavior.

Note, though, that Dimmesdale cannot convince even himself that he is right in not confessing that he and Hester had an affair and that Pearl is the child of that affair. He knows it is wrong not to confess and repent – but he simply cannot bring himself to do so. There are times in his sermons when he comes to the brink of confessing, but he always stops short. He hates himself for his inability to confess. Thus, he punishes himself. He takes a whip and lashes himself until he is bloody. He allows Chillingworth to make him feel guilty until he almost goes crazy. His sense of guilt consumes him, and his anguish increases when he sees Hester suffering alone for the sin which he committed with her.

Perhaps the real reason that Dimmesdale cannot confess is this: he is a weak man. He doesn't want to admit that he sinned against the Puritan God whom he serves. He yearns to be perfect, and obviously he was – until his moment of passion with Hester. He hates himself for that sin, and he hates himself even more because he cannot acknowledge his sin publicly and then repent. For this reason, we realize that after seven long years of struggle, Dimmesdale accomplishes victory over his weakness – and he is also victorious over his weakness on the very day that should have been his greatest triumph as a stainless man of God. That day he delivers a magnificent sermon, and afterward, he confesses on the scaffold to his sin.

Chillingworth's remarks show the importance of Dimmesdale's confession: "Hadst thou sought the whole earth over, there was no place so secret – no high place nor lowly place where thou couldst have escaped me – save on this very scaffold!" In fact, Hawthorne himself in his "Conclusion" specifically points out his intended meaning: "Among many morals which press upon us from the poor minister's miserable experience, we put only this into a sentence: 'Be true! Be true! Be true! Show freely to the world, if not your worst, yet some trait whereby the worst may be inferred!'"

In many ways, *The Scarlet Letter* is Dimmesdale's story. The central struggle is his. Whereas the other characters occupy relatively fixed positions, the minister must – in one dramatic decision – reverse his actions of seven years' time. And that reversal marks his victory over himself and marks the climax of the novel.

Roger Chillingworth

When Chillingworth first appears, having just ended over a year's captivity by the Indians, his appearance is hideous, partly because of his strange mixture of "civilized and savage costume." But even when he is better dressed, he is far from attractive. He is small, thin, and slightly deformed, with one shoulder higher than the other. Although he "could hardly be termed aged," he has a wrinkled face and appears "well stricken in years." He has, however, a look of calm intelligence, and his eyes, though they have a "strange, penetrating power," are dim and bleared, testifying to long hours of study under lamplight. He has, indeed, spent his life as a lonely scholar, cutting himself off from the world of other men in his quest for knowledge. Even after his marriage to Hester, he spent most of his time alone in his study. The areas of his knowledge are not defined, but among them are alchemy (which is more closely related to magic than it is to science) and medicine (although he is not a licensed physician, he is "a better physician . . . than many that claim the medical degree").

At first, Chillingworth appears to be more sinned against than sinning. After all, he has been held captive by the Indians for over a year, and when he returns to civilization, he sees his wife, standing on the scaffold of Boston, holding a baby that is not his, but his wife's lover's baby. Remember, Chillingworth (whose real name is Roger Prynne) has not seen his wife for over two years, and now she stands before him holding in her arms the child of another man.

But before the novel has ended, Chillingworth will be deeply guilty of not one sin but two – one which leads almost inevitably to the other sins of the novel, and a second which is far more awful than the sins of either Hester or Dimmesdale.

Chillingworth's first sin is one against Nature. He committed it the day he married his young, passionate wife. He knew that Hester did not love him, and that he was not the kind of man to make her a proper husband. He was not deliberately wronging anybody; there is even pathos in his recollection (Chapter 4): "It seemed not so wild a dream,—old as I was, and sombre as I was, and misshapen as I was,—that the simple bliss, which is scattered far and wide, for all mankind to gather up, might yet be mine. And so, Hester, I drew thee into my heart, into its innermost chamber, and sought to warm thee by the warmth which thy presence made there!"

Ignorance, however, does not excuse Chillingworth's selfish desire to have a lovely young wife. And one should remember that Chillingworth was largely ignorant about other people. He hadn't been around them; he had immersed himself in his studies. But he knows now that he was wrong to marry a woman who did not love him. He did sin, and he knows it: "Mine was the first wrong, when I betrayed thy budding youth into a false and unnatural relation with my decay." And Hester knows it too (Chapter 15): "It seemed a fouler offence committed by Roger Chillingworth, than any which had since been done him, that, in the time when her heart knew no better, he had persuaded her to fancy herself happy by his side."

But far worse than that offense is the sin which begins to take possession of Chillingworth when he first appears at the scaffold scene. Briefly defined, this sin is the subordination of the heart to the intellect. It occurs when one is willing to sacrifice his fellow man to gratify his own selfish interests. As displayed in Chillingworth, it involves a violation of two biblical injunctions: (1) "Judge not, that ye be not judged" and (2) "Vengeance is mine, saith the Lord."

Chillingworth does indeed judge Dimmesdale, and Chillingworth is so intent on taking vengeance that he spends his waking hours trying to destroy the minister's sanity. But, as is typical of this sin—Hawthorne called it "the unpardonable sin"—Chillingworth eventually destroys himself. He tries to play God and, instead, he metamorphoses himself into a devil.

By Chapter 9, the change in Chillingworth is apparent: "A large number . . . affirmed that Roger Chillingworth's aspect had undergone a remarkable change while he had dwelt in town, and especially since his abode with Mr. Dimmesdale. At first, his expression had been calm, meditative, scholar-like. Now, there was something ugly and evil in his face, which they had not previously noticed, and which grew still the more obvious to sight the oftener they looked upon him." Chapter 10 develops this idea more fully, as it shows the manner in which Chillingworth works on Dimmesdale while pretending to be his friend and physician. By Chapter 14, Chillingworth's transformation into a devil appears to be complete.

Chillingworth is aware of what has happened, and he says to Hester: "Dost thou remember me? Was I not, though you might deem me cold, nevertheless a man thoughtful for others, craving little for himself, – kind, true, just, and of constant, if not warm affections? . . . And what am I now? . . . I have already told thee what I am! A fiend! Who made me so?!"

Chillingworth's question is rhetorical – that is, he doesn't ask it for an answer. He *knows* the answer – he thinks. He thinks that Dimmesdale made him into a fiend; Dimmesdale is the one responsible. Hester, however, immediately accepts the blame herself. But for Hawthorne, and for us, neither of those answers will do. Chillingworth must assume the responsibility for having destroyed himself. It is he who has sacrificed his human sympathies in his desire for revenge.

This particular point is made specifically in Chapter 17, when Dimmesdale says to Hester: "We are not, Hester, the worst sinners in the world. There is one worse than even the polluted priest [a reference to Dimmesdale himself]! That old man's revenge [Chillingworth's] has been blacker than my sin. He has violated, in cold blood, the sanctity of a human heart. Thou and I, Hester, never did so!"

In the concluding chapter, when Hawthorne speaks of Chillingworth's withering up and shriveling away, he makes it plain that the physician's fate was the most horrible of the three because his sin was the blackest.

Pearl

Pearl appears first as an infant, then at the age of three, and finally at the age of seven. The fullest description of her comes in Chapter 6. There, we see her at the age of three. We learn that she possesses a "rich and luxuriant beauty; a beauty that shone with deep and vivid tints; a bright complexion, eyes possessing intensity both of depth and glow, and hair already of a deep, glossy brown and which, in after years, would be nearly akin to black."

We learn further that Pearl has a "perfect shape," "vigor," "natural dexterity," and "a native grace," and that in public she is usually dressed in "gorgeous robes which might have extinguished a paler loveliness." This is not a very detailed picture Hawthorne has provided, but if he is rather vague about Pearl's physical appearance, he goes to great lengths to convey her personality.

Pearl is intelligent, imaginative, inquisitive, determined, and even obstinate at times. She is a baffling mixture of strong moods, given to uncontrolled laughter at one moment and sullen silence the next, with a fierce temper and a capacity for the "bitterest hatred that can be supposed to rankle in a childish bosom." So unusual is her behavior that she is often referred to in such terms as "elf-child," "imp," and "airy sprite." Governor Bellingham likens her to the "children of the Lord of Misrule," and some of the Puritans believe that she is a "demon offspring."

One may perhaps attribute much of Pearl's strangeness to a combination of her exceptional quickness of mind and the abnormal environment in which she is reared, with only her mother as a companion. But certainly, there is something otherworldly about her until the events of Chapter 23 bring her fully into the world of humanity. This is part of Hawthorne's design. He is not attempting to realistically develop a "normal" little girl. Throughout the book, he is using Pearl as a symbol, and as a symbol, Pearl is one of his most remarkable creations.

From the beginning of the novel, Pearl is an obvious symbol of the illicit love affair between Hester and Dimmesdale. Hester realizes that fact in Chapter 2, when she resists the temptation to hold Pearl in front of the scarlet *A*, "wisely judging that one token of her shame would but poorly serve to hide another." But Pearl soon becomes more than a mere token of sin. Hawthorne begins to elaborate on Pearl as a symbol in Chapter 4, when he tells us that the infant "writhed in convulsions of pain, and was a forcible type in its little frame." Here, Hawthorne focuses on the agony which Hester Prynne has experienced throughout this long and trying day.

As Pearl develops a personality, she becomes symbolic of the kind of passion that accompanied Hester's sin. Chapter 6 develops this point at length. There we read: "Hester could only account for the child's character – and even then most vaguely and imperfectly – by recalling what she herself had been, during that momentous period while Pearl was imbibing her soul from the spiritual world, and her bodily frame from its material of earth. The mother's impassioned state had been the medium through which were transmitted to the unborn infant the rays of its moral life; and, however white and clear originally, they had taken the deep stains of crimson and gold, the fiery lustre, the black shadow, and the untempered light of the intervening substance. Above all, the warfare of Hester's spirit, at that epoch, was perpetuated in Pearl."

The fact that Pearl can see and talk and show emotion helps Hawthorne to make her an active and forceful symbol. From the first time that she notices the scarlet A on her mother's breast, Pearl is not merely a passive reminder of sin. Rather, she plays an active (even if unknowing) role in Hester's punishment. In Chapter 6, we read: "But that first object of which Pearl seemed to become aware was – shall we say it? – the scarlet letter on Hester's bosom! One day, as her mother stooped over the cradle, the infant's eyes had been caught by the glimmering of the gold embroidery about the letter; and, putting up her little hand, she grasped at it, smiling not doubtfully, but with a decided gleam, that gave her face the look of a much older child."

As Pearl grows older, her actions and her questions are matters of increasing torment to Hester. Pearl pelts the scarlet letter with flowers, "covering the mother's breast with hurts for which she could find no balm in this world," and then she adds to Hester's pain by demanding to know where she "came from," and by refusing to accept Hester's biblical explanation that Pearl's Heavenly Father sent her (Chapter 6). When the breastplate at Governor Bellingham's mansion distorts the scarlet A into something overpowering and horrible, it is Pearl who points at it, "smiling at her mother, with the elfish intelligence that was so familiar an expression on her small physiognomy" (Chapter 7).

Pearl's tendency to focus on the scarlet letter is fully developed in Chapter 15, where Pearl mimics her mother by placing a seaweed A on her own breast, and then, with her repeated questions regarding the letter's significance, she finally forces Hester to deny the significance of the letter.

On their forest walk, Pearl observes to Hester that "the sunshine does not love you. It runs away and hides itself, because it is afraid of something on your bosom" (Chapter 16). And, finally, in one of the book's most dramatic scenes, it is Pearl who blocks her mother's attempted escape from her symbol of shame. In the woods, after Hester has thrown her scarlet letter to the ground, Pearl shrieks in a fit of passion and will not come to her mother until Hester puts the scarlet *A* back on and tucks her hair under her cap once again (Chapter 19).

As Pearl thus becomes so closely associated with the letter *A* on Hester's breast, becoming, as Hawthorne says in Chapter 7, "the scarlet letter in another form; the scarlet letter endowed with life," she becomes the embodiment not only of Hester's sin, but of her conscience. She is a far stronger device for punishing Hester than is the piece of cloth on Hester's bosom. And, because it is through Hester's acceptance of punishment that she is saved, Pearl becomes the chief agent in her mother's salvation. This insight is supported by Hester's declaration to Mistress Hibbins in Chapter 8: "Had they taken her from me, I would willingly have gone with thee into the forest, and signed my name in the Black Man's book too, and that with mine own blood!"

But it is not only toward Hester that Pearl functions as a symbol. To Dimmesdale also, Pearl becomes a kind of living conscience. As early as the first scaffold scene (Chapter 3), when Dimmesdale is ironically calling on Hester to reveal the name of the infant's father, Pearl's actions take on symbolic significance: "The poor baby . . . directed its hitherto vacant gaze towards Mr. Dimmesdale, and held up its little arms, with a half-pleased, half-plaintive murmur." Pearl, of course, does not understand the implications of that action, but, to Dimmesdale, the reaching out toward him must be painfully significant. He is, after all, a man denying his own flesh-and-blood daughter.

As she grows older, Pearl makes her appeal for recognition again and again, and in more specific terms. In the central scaffold scene, she asks Dimmesdale, "Wilt thou stand here with mother and me, to-morrow noontide?" Dimmesdale refuses, and Pearl attempts to pull away her hand. She makes the request again. A few minutes later, she complains, "Thou was not bold! – thou wast not true! . . . Thou wouldst not promise to take my hand, and my mother's hand, to-morrow noontide!"

Again in Chapter 19, in the forest after Hester has told Pearl that Dimmesdale loves them, Pearl insists on his public recognition of them: "Will he go back with us, hand in hand, we three together, into the town?" When it is made plain that he will not, Pearl washes away his kiss and then remains apart from the two adults.

As Hester is describing the approaching Election Day procession in Chapter 21, Pearl again repeats her request for Dimmesdale's recognition: "And will he hold out both his hands to me, as when thou ledst me to him from the brook-side?" After the procession has passed, Pearl remarks that had she recognized Dimmesdale, she would have demanded his recognition: "I would have run to him, and bid him kiss me now, before all the people. . . . Would he have clapped his hand over his heart, and scowled on me, and bid me be gone?"

It is true that Pearl herself cannot understand the full implications of her questions. It is equally true, however, that what she repeatedly requests Dimmesdale to do is the very thing that he *must do* in order to save his soul. Dimmesdale must, in public and in broad daylight, acknowledge his relationship to Hester and Pearl. In the final scaffold scene, he finally does take that crucial step, and Pearl's function as a symbol has been completed: "Pearl kissed his lips. A spell was broken. The great scene of grief in which the wild infant bore a part, had developed all her sympathies; and as her tears fell upon her father's cheek, they were the pledge that she would grow up amid human joy and sorrow, nor forever do battle with the world, but be a woman in it. Towards her mother, too, Pearl's errand as a messenger of anguish was all fulfilled."

CRITICAL ESSAYS

HAWTHORNE AND *THE SCARLET LETTER*

Although Hawthorne wrote to his friend Bridges that he thought *The House of the Seven Gables* was a better book than *The Scarlet Letter*, most modern critics consider *The Scarlet Letter* to be his masterpiece. In fact, evidence of the continued popularity of this work, even among people not usually concerned with literary works, appeared in two 1984 issues of the *New England Journal of Medicine*.

Jemshed A. Kahn, a physician, suggested that Dimmesdale was a victim of atropine poisoning, administered by Chillingworth. He supports his claim by citing Hawthorne's mention of plants which contain the poison, and he concludes that the symptoms experienced by Dimmesdale – the hallucinations, the convulsions, the tremors, and the "red stigmata of guilt," which some witnesses described as being on Dimmesdale's chest at the close of the novel – are all consistent with the known symptoms of atropine poisoning. Three months later, the same journal carried a series of letters both in praise of – and critical of – Khan's views. That such a furor could be generated among present-day readers by a novel written more than a hundred and thirty years ago is ample testimony to the power of Hawthorne's novel and its continuing popularity.

In an entirely different vein, yet one that is worth investigating, one should consider a theory recently advanced by another scholar. Hawthorne, as noted, was always concerned with his family history and with colonial history. His earliest American ancestor, William Hathorne, arrived in this country with John Winthrop, later governor of the Massachusetts Bay Colony, in 1630. Hathorne became the Speaker of the House of Delegates and was also a major in the Salem militia. This "steeple-crowned progenitor" who "had all the Puritanic traits, both good and evil," was remembered by the Quakers for an "incident of his hard severity towards a woman of their sect." Even Hawthorne thought that the memory of his ancestor's severity toward the woman would "last longer, it is to be feared, than any record of his better deeds."

William's son, John, became even more famous – or infamous. He was one of the three judges in the Salem witchcraft trials of 1692. It is he who is mentioned in the "Custom House" section of *The Scarlet Letter* as having "made himself so conspicuous in the martyrdom of the witches, that their blood may fairly be said to have left a stain upon him." Hawthorne's reaction to the early history of these two ancestors may well have led him to declare that "I, the present writer, as their representative, hereby take shame upon myself for their sakes, and pray that any curse incurred by them . . . may be now and henceforth removed."

For many readers, the shame which Hawthorne took upon himself, as a result of the actions of his paternal ancestors, has been enough to account for what he designates as one of the "many morals" which Dimmesdale's experience might provide for the reader. That moral is placed by Hawthorne in the final chapter of the novel where he writes, "Be true! Be true! Show freely to the world, if not your worst, yet some trait whereby the worst may be inferred!" Interestingly, as mentioned earlier, a number of scholars have looked further into Hawthorne's family history, past the apparent "sins" of his paternal ancestors, believing that the witch-hunting fervor of these long-dead relatives was not a sufficient cause of Hawthorne's strong protest for us to "show . . . if not [the] worst, yet some trait whereby the worst may be inferred!" They have sought elsewhere for a possible explanation for the fevered moral which Hawthorne makes so impassionately.

For example, in 1984, the critic Philip Young published *Hawthorne's Secret*, arguing that Hawthorne quite probably uncovered a bit of startling information related to his maternal ancestors that would account for the impassioned moral in the last chapter of *The Scarlet Letter*.

In the "Quarterly Court Records" of Essex Country, Massachusetts, Hawthorne may well have found the records of a court case which took place on March 29, 1681. Two of Hawthorne's maternal ancestors, Anstis and Margaret Manning, were convicted of having committed incest with their brother, Nicholas. They were sentenced to be publicly whipped and to stand in the middle of the Salem meeting house with a paper on their heads revealing the nature of their crime. The substitution of an adulterous for an incestuous relationship could indeed be a case of showing "some trait whereby the worst may be inferred."

This sort of scholarly research can hardly be said to provide absolute proof that Hawthorne was aware of that particular aspect of his ancestors' history, but it does again demonstrate that there is still a great interest in *The Scarlet Letter* and in Hawthorne's motivations for writing it.

As one considers those two recent speculations, one should also consider more mundane, but certainly valuable aspects of Hawthorne's masterpiece. It is important, for example, to know that when Hawthorne finished *The Scarlet Letter*, he had already written most of the works that were to make him famous. Thus, many of the stylistic techniques and themes which are characteristic of a work by Hawthorne were already a habitual part of his style. Those elements include: (1) Hawthorne's theory of the romance as a literary form; (2) Hawthorne's use of symbolism in the novel; (3) Hawthorne's style; (4) Hawthorne's use of historical materials and figures as part of the setting; and, finally, (5) Hawthorne's use of ambiguity.

HAWTHORNE AND THE ROMANCE TRADITION

Although many critics use the terms *symbol* and *symbolist* when they are discussing Hawthorne's writing techniques and the nature of his work, these are not terms which Hawthorne would have understood as we use them today. He would have described his technique as that of a writer using allegory, and he would have described the novels which he wrote as "romances."

During his writing career, Hawthorne was convinced that his works were not as popular as they might have been, and he attributed this lack of popularity to what he called allegories. In an 1854 introduction, published with "Rappaccini's Daughter," he wrote that his books "might have won him a greater reputation but for an inveterate love of allegory, which is apt to invest plots and characters with the aspect of scenery and people in the clouds and to steal the human warmth of his conceptions."

One should note, however, that Hawthorne would have considered the term *allegories* to include any work that used fictional materials and devices to develop an idea or to convey a moral. In fact, he would have considered all but a very few of his tales to be allegories. This technique, or style, developed throughout his longer works, produced his version of what he termed "the romance novel."

Convinced that his "native land," as he termed it, contained few readers who could truly appreciate the romance as a literary form, Hawthorne attempted to explain why this was the case. In his preface to *The Marble Faun* (1869), he commented, "It will be very long, I trust, before romance writers may find congenial and easily handled themes, either in the annals of our stalwart republic, or in any characteristic and probable events of our individual lives." Hawthorne felt that America was "a country where there is no shadow, no antiquity, no mystery, no picturesque and gloomy wrong, nor anything but a commonplace prosperity, in broad and simple daylight, as is happily the case with my dear native land."

In his preface to *The Blithedale Romance* (1852), Hawthorne notes that in the old countries the writer of romances was "allowed a license with regard to every-day probability in view of the improved effects which he is bound to produce thereby." Because New World readers seemed to demand a more realistic writing style than romance offered, the writer of romances was often placed at a disadvantage. Lacking an audience which would accept what Hawthorne called a "faery-land, so like the real world, that, in a suitable remoteness, one cannot well tell the difference, but with an atmosphere of strange enchantment, beheld through which the inhabitants have a propriety of their own," the writer of romances was forced to write in such a way that the results were sometimes less than satisfactory. To satisfy the tastes of New World readers, "the beings of imagination are compelled to show themselves in the same category as actually living mortals; a necessity that generally renders the paint and pasteboard of their composition but too painfully discernible."

Convinced, however, that the romance was the style most congenial to his purposes, Hawthorne often attempted to explain, and at some length, the distinction which he made between the romance and the novel. One key paragraph where he attempts to make this distinction is found in his preface to *The House of the Seven Gables* (1851):

When a writer calls his work a Romance, it need hardly be observed that he wishes to claim a latitude, both as to its fashion and material, which he would not have felt himself entitled to assume had he professed to be writing a Novel. The latter form of composition is presumed to aim at a very minute fidelity, not merely to the possible, but to the probable and ordinary course of man's experience. The former— while, as a work of art, it must rigidly subject itself to laws, and while it sins unpardonably so far as it may swerve aside from the truth of the human heart—has fairly a right to present that truth under circumstances, to a great extent, of the writer's own choosing or creation. If he think fit, also, he may so manage his atmospherical material as to bring out or mellow the lights and deepen and enrich the shadows of the picture.

Another of Hawthorne's attempts to clarify his concept of the romance is found in the "Custom House" section of *The Scarlet Letter* (1850). Shortly after having explained how he, supposedly, by accident, found a scarlet letter *A* and a "small roll of dingy paper," around which the scarlet letter had been twisted, Hawthorne presents an explanation of what he takes to be the frame of mind necessary for presenting such a story to the public. Using the image of a "deserted parlour, lighted only by the glimmering coal-fire and the moon," Hawthorne outlines the frame of mind necessary for both writing and for reading his romance.

> Moonlight . . . making every object so minutely visible, yet so unlike a morning or noontide visibility, – is a medium the most suited for a romance-writer to get acquainted with his illusive guests. . . . all these details [objects in the room], so completely seen, are so spiritualized by the unusual light, that they seem to lose their actual substance and become things of the intellect. . . . Thus, therefore, the floor of our familiar room has become a neutral territory, somewhere between the real world and fairy-land, where the Actual and the Imaginary may meet, and each imbue itself with the nature of the other. . . . The somewhat dim coal-fire has an essential influence in producing the effect which I would describe. . . . This warmer light mingles itself with the cold spirituality of the moonbeams, and communicates, as it were, a heart and sensibilities of human tenderness to the forms which fancy summons up. It converts them from snow images into men and women. Glancing at the looking-glass, we behold – deep within its haunted verge – the smouldering glow of the half-extinguished anthracite, the white moonbeams on the floor, and a repetition of all the gleam and shadow of the picture, with one remove farther from the actual, and nearer to the imagination. Then, at such an hour, and with this scene before him, if a man, sitting all alone, cannot dream strange things, and make them look like truth, he need never try to write romances.

If one examines these statements of Hawthorne and evaluates them in the light of his customary themes and concerns, one might conclude that he was attempting to plumb below the visible surface of the world in which he lived and examine the roots and well-springs of human conduct.

HAWTHORNE'S SYMBOLISM

Generally speaking, a symbol is something which is used to stand for something else. In literature, it is most often a concrete object which is used to represent something more abstract and broader in scope and meaning – often a moral, religious, or philosophical concept or value. Symbols can range from the most obvious substitution of one thing for another, to creations as massive, complex, and perplexing as Melville's white whale in *Moby-Dick*.

In Hawthorne's use of symbols in *The Scarlet Letter,* we observe the author making one of his most distinctive and significant contributions to the growth of American fiction. Indeed, this novel is usually regarded as the first symbolic novel to be published in the United States.

Several of Hawthorne's many symbols in *The Scarlet Letter* are obvious. In the first chapter, for example, he describes the prison as "the black flower of civilized society"; by using the building of the prison to represent the crime and the punishment which were aspects of early Boston's civilized life, and by contrasting this symbol with the tombstone at the end of the novel, he appears to be suggesting that crime and cruel punishment may well bring about the death of civilized life.

In the same chapter, he uses the grass plot "much overgrown with burdock, pigweed, apple-peru, and such unsightly vegetation" as another symbol of civilization corrupted by the elements which make prisons necessary. He also points out another symbol, this one a positive symbol, in the wild rosebush. He says that "it may serve . . . to symbolize some sweet moral blossom, that may be found along the track, or relieve the darkening close of a tale of human frailty and sorrow."

Shortly afterward, in Chapter 2, Hawthorne uses the beadle ("like a black shadow . . . grim and grisly . . . with a sword by his side, and his staff of office in his hand") as a symbol for Puritanism, in general.

These symbols are easy to find. More impressive, however, are the symbols which Hawthorne sustains throughout the novel, allowing each of them to develop and take on various appearances and meanings as the book progresses. Among such symbols is the letter *A* itself. In its initial form, it is a red cloth letter which is a literal symbol of the sin of adultery. But Hawthorne makes the *A* much more richly symbolic before the novel ends.

The letter *A* appears in a variety of forms and places. It is the elaborately gold-embroidered *A* on Hester's heart, at which Pearl throws wildflowers (Chapter 6). It is magnified in the armor breastplate at Governor Bellingham's mansion, seen "in exaggerated and gigantic proportions, so as to be greatly the most prominent feature of her appearance. In truth, she seemed absolutely hidden behind it" (Chapter 7).

Later, the *A* on Hester's breast is decorated by Pearl with a border of "prickly burrs from a tall burdock which grew beside the tomb" (Chapter 10). On the night of his vigil on the scaffold, Dimmesdale sees an immense red *A* in the sky (Chapter 12). While Hester is conferring with Chillingworth near the bay shore, Pearl arranges eel-grass to form a green *A* on her own breast (Chapter 15). One of the most dramatic of the several *A*'s in the book is the *A* so frequently hinted at earlier and which is finally revealed to be an *A* on Dimmesdale's chest by "most of the spectators" (Chapter 24) who witnessed his confession and death (Chapter 23). At the very end of the novel, as a kind of summary symbol, there is the reference to the scarlet *A* against the black background on Hester and Dimmesdale's tombstone (Chapter 24).

Not only does the *A* appear in various forms, but it also acquires a variety of meanings. Even as the original mark of adultery, the scarlet letter has different personal meanings to the various characters. To the Puritan community, it is a mark of just punishment. To Hester, the *A* is a symbol of unjust humiliation. To Dimmesdale, the *A* is a piercing reminder of his own guilt. To Chillingworth, the *A* is a spur to the quest for revenge. To Pearl, the *A* is a bright and mysterious curiosity. In addition, the *A* also symbolizes things other than adultery. For example, it symbolizes "Angel" when it appears in the sky on the night of Governor Winthrop's death (Chapter 12), and it symbolizes "Able" when, years after her humiliation on the scaffold, Hester has won some respect from the Puritans (Chapter 13).

Many of the other sustained or important symbols in the novel lie either in the setting or in the characters. The scaffold, for instance, is not only a symbol of the stern Puritan code, but it also becomes a symbol for the open acknowledgment of personal sin. It is also the place to which Dimmesdale knows he must go for atonement, the only place where he can escape the grasp of Chillingworth.

Night is used as a symbol for concealment, and day is a symbol for exposure. Dimmesdale's mounting the scaffold and standing with

Hester and Pearl at night will not suffice; he knows that his symbolic acceptance of his guilt must take place in the daylight.

The sun is also used as a symbol of untroubled, guilt-free happiness, or perhaps the approval of God and nature. The sun shines on Pearl, even in the forest; she seems to absorb and retain the sunshine. But the sun flees from Hester and from the mark of sin on her breast. The forest itself is symbolic in a variety of ways. It is a place where witches gather, where souls are signed away to the devil, and where Dimmesdale can "yield himself with deliberate choice . . . to what he knew was deadly sin." It is a symbol, then, of the world of darkness and evil.

In addition, it also symbolizes a place where Pearl can run and play freely, a friend of the animals and the wild flowers, and where even Hester can throw away her scarlet *A*, let down her hair, and feel like a woman again. It is also symbolic of a natural world governed by natural laws—as opposed to the artificial, strict community with its man-made Puritan laws (Chapter 18).

The forest also symbolizes a place where darkness and gloom predominate and where one can find his way only by following a narrow, twisting path; it is a symbol of the "moral wilderness" in which Hester has been wandering (Chapter 16).

The brook in the forest is also symbolic in several ways. First, it is suggestive of Pearl—because of its unknown source and because it travels through gloom. Because of its mournful babble, it becomes a kind of history of sorrow, to which one more story is added. And when Pearl refuses to cross the brook to join Hester and Dimmesdale, the brook becomes (to Dimmesdale) a "boundary between two worlds" (Chapter 19). The natural setting, then, provides many of the most striking symbols in the novel.

But perhaps the most revealing display of Hawthorne's symbolism lies in his use of characters. His minor characters are almost wholly symbolic. The Puritan notions of Church, State, and Witchcraft are personified in the figures of the Reverend Mr. Wilson, Governor Bellingham, and Mistress Hibbins. It is interesting to note that Hawthorne mentions all three of them in connection with each of the scaffold scenes. The groups of unnamed somber and self-righteous Puritans in the marketplace (Chapters 21–23) are clearly representative of Puritanism generally, even down to the detail of the gentle young wife who saves Hawthorne's condemnation of the Puritans from being a complete one.

It is, however, in the four major characters that Hawthorne's powers as a symbolist are brought into fullest play. Each of his major characters symbolizes a certain view of sin and its effects on the human heart. And one of them, Pearl, is almost a self-contained symbol – perhaps the most striking symbol that Hawthorne ever created.

HAWTHORNE'S STYLE

The style of *The Scarlet Letter* is clean, precise, and effective. Hawthorne's vocabulary is wide and well controlled. He wrote at a formal level – that is, he avoided ungrammatical expressions, slang, vulgarisms, colloquialisms, and profanity. He chose his words with a sharp sense of precise meaning, and he had a keen ear for euphony, or pleasant sounds. While reading this novel, one may occasionally have to consult a dictionary, but more often than not, the word in question will be a word which was in standard usage in 1850, but has become obsolete since that time. During Hawthorne's own time, his prose was extraordinarily precise. It was not overly ornate, as it sometimes might seem to today's readers.

Hawthorne's style is also noteworthy because of his frequent use of images. Metaphors and similes abound in the novel, most of them strikingly fresh and effective, and he makes skillful use of colors – from the red rose of the opening chapter to the red and black tombstone of his final sentence. In fact, the colors red, black, and gray predominate in this novel. Their effectiveness in creating the mood and supporting the meaning of the novel is apparent to anyone who has read the book carefully.

The chief fault to be found in Hawthorne's language is that it tends to be too consistently the same, whether inside quotation marks or not. The characters, when they speak, all sound essentially like Hawthorne, and although the characters are quite different in their ages, their educations, their personalities, and their backgrounds, it is almost impossible to tell them apart from the manner of their speech. This failure to individualize the dialogue, or to make the speech consistent with the character and situation of the speaker, is a weakness which later novelists tried to avoid.

HISTORICAL MATERIALS AND FIGURES

As Hawthorne indicates in the "Custom House" chapter of *The Scarlet Letter*, two of his ancestors were eminent and powerful men during the early days of the Massachusetts Bay Colony. One was a magistrate who participated in the persecution of the Quakers, and another was a judge in the infamous Salem witch trials. Because of this family association, Hawthorne had a keen interest in the early history of Massachusetts, and from his college days on, he read widely in that field. This fact, coupled with his relative aloofness from matters of his own day, makes it no surprise that he should choose the historical setting of Puritan Massachusetts for his masterpiece.

The Scarlet Letter, however, is not a historical novel in the strict sense of the term, and the historical setting, if examined closely, is rather thinly developed. Hawthorne is obviously more interested in conveying some timeless and universal truths about sin and conscience and psychology than he is in relating minutely accurate information about a specific time and a specific place.

The place of the action, as Hawthorne tells us in the opening chapter, is Boston, the seat of government for the Massachusetts Bay Colony. The time can be fixed quite accurately from Hawthorne's hints. The opening of Chapter 2 indicates that the story begins "not less than two centuries ago." Using the date of Hawthorne's writing, that would make the time of the novel's opening pages about 1650, or perhaps a bit earlier. The reference in Chapter 12 to Governor Winthrop's death provides an even more exact clue. Winthrop died in 1649, and inasmuch as Pearl is seven years old at the time of Winthrop's death, the novel clearly opens in 1642.

There are also some other incidental historical allusions in the book which make it evident that Hawthorne was quite familiar with the period about which he writes: the use of Governor Bellingham and the Reverend Mr. Wilson; the passing reference to Isaac Johnson's lot, King's Chapel, Prison Lane, Anne Hutchinson, John Eliot, Increase Mather, and a handful of other historical figures. The detailed treatment of Puritan methods of punishment, as well as Hawthorne's description of the Election Day crowd are superbly described with historical accuracy.

Hawthorne is generally credited with having caught the mood and the spirit of early American Puritanism, but he has certainly not attempted to give us a detailed account of the cultural, social, domestic, or political aspects of the historical period of *The Scarlet Letter*. For example, there is no information about the houses in which the Puritans lived, the jobs they held, the food they ate, the implements they used, or the books they read. We learn virtually nothing about their family customs, their recreation, or their educational system. In fact, only twice does Hawthorne make any real attempt to illuminate the minute details of the life of that historical period. In Chapter 7, however, he does give us a rather detailed description of Governor Bellingham's mansion and its furnishings. Similarly, in Chapter 11, he gives us some details about the Puritans' clothing and the general facial expressions of the people, as well as some indications of their popular public recreations.

It might be argued that Hawthorne's failure to detail the general mode of life of that era results from the fact that his four characters are more or less isolated from the community and that he has little occasion to treat the details of general community life. Note, however, that although Hester and Pearl spend seven years quite closely confined to their little cottage, the reader sees not one article of furniture, nor any book, curtain, ornament, or dish inside that house.

Hawthorne was *not* a realist. He was a symbolist. He selected from the village (and from the countryside which surrounds it) those details which would best help him to set the mood and convey his ideas. Because the scaffold, the forest, Mistress Hibbins, Governor Bellingham, the Election Sermon, the drab and solemn townspeople, and even the period itself was useful to his purpose, he uses these with strong symbolic precision. By allowing himself this latitude in his choice of details, Hawthorne is able to mellow the lights, deepening and enriching the shadows of the world of *The Scarlet Letter*.

HAWTHORNE AND THE USE OF AMBIGUITY

Hawthorne's use of ambiguity or, as the critic F. O. Matthiessen has called it, "multiple choice," is employed several times in *The Scarlet Letter*. It is, however, a device which has its origins in a number of Hawthorne's earlier stories. With this device, Hawthorne casts doubt on his own story as he has told it, and he suggests that an incident may have happened in quite a different way, if at all.

Readers familiar with "Young Goodman Brown" (1835) or "The

Minister's Black Veil" (1836) may well recall several obvious uses of the device in those early stories. The staff of the gentleman whom Brown meets in the forest is described as having ". . . the likeness of a great black snake, so curiously wrought that it might almost be seen to twist and wriggle itself, like a living serpent." At this point, Hawthorne adds, "This must have been an oracular deception, assisted by the uncertain light." In addition, even the ending of the story is presented in such a way that the "common-sensible man" (as Hawthorne called him) can reject the supernatural elements of the story if he so wishes. "Had Goodman Brown fallen asleep in the forest," Hawthorne says, "and only dreamed a wild dream of a witch-meeting? Be it so if you will. But alas! it was a dream of evil omen for young Goodman Brown."

In "The Minister's Black Veil," the corpse of a young woman over whom the clergyman leaned was reported to have "slightly shuddered" when the minister's face was revealed to her. Hawthorne immediately adds, however, "A superstitious old woman was the only witness of this prodigy."

Turning to *The Scarlet Letter,* one finds that Hawthorne continued to use this device of ambiguity to defuse the skeptical objections of his "common-sensible" readers. At the end of Chapter 8, while discussing the significance of Hester's conversation with Mistress Hibbins, Hawthorne inserts this qualifying phrase: ". . . if we suppose this interview betwixt Mistress Hibbins and Hester Prynne to be authentic, and not a parable." In Chapter 12, while describing the scarlet *A* which Dimmesdale (and according to the sexton and others as well) saw in the sky, Hawthorne remarks: "We impart it . . . solely to the disease in his own eye and heart, that the minister, looking upward to the zenith, beheld there the appearance of an immense letter, – the letter *A*, – marked out in lines of dull red light."

When telling how the forest animals befriended Pearl, in Chapter 18, Hawthorne writes: "A wolf, it is said, – but here the tale has surely lapsed into the improbable, – came up and smelt of Pearl's robe and offered his savage head to be patted by her hand." Again, in Chapter 20, Hawthorne qualifies his discussion of Dimmesdale's interview with Mistress Hibbins, noting skeptically, ". . . if it were a real incident." But the most striking use of the optional reading comes in Chapter 24, where Hawthorne lists the various interpretations, all by eyewitnesses, of Dimmesdale's final actions and of the letter *A* on his chest. Some observers (on whose opinion Hawthorne casts doubt) even assert that there was no letter, nor any confession.

In all of these cases, Hawthorne leaves the solution to the reader; the reader must decide what is "literally true." It seems as if Hawthorne wishes to make use of the supernatural or fantastic devices for symbols, but also offers an optional explanation for the literal-minded reader to whom the fantastic is not justified — not even for an artistic effect. Actually, Hawthorne's method of narration gives him the best of two worlds. He is somewhat like the trial lawyer who withdraws a telling remark upon the judge's objection, but knows that the implications of his remark will remain in the minds of the jury members.

SUGGESTED ESSAY TOPICS

Short Essays

1. Justify Hawthorne's including "The Custom House" preface as part of the novel.

2. Discuss how Hawthorne uses the setting in Chapter 1 to set the mood for the novel.

3. What is the function of the "Conclusion"? What is its effect on the unity and on the general artistic quality of the novel?

4. How does Hawthorne employ the forest as a symbol?

5. What is meant by the term "type character"? To what extent are Hawthorne's major characters "types"?

6. Discuss the function of the following minor characters: (1) Mistress Hibbins, (2) Governor Bellingham, and (3) Mr. Wilson.

7. Show in what ways Pearl's behavior seems unnatural or abnormal. What facts may account for that abnormality? At what point in the book does she undergo a change, and why?

Long Essays

1. Discuss the unity of place and the unity of time in *The Scarlet Letter*.

2. Discuss Hawthorne's style, its strengths and its weaknesses.

3. Discuss the significance of the three scaffold scenes.

4. To what degree does Hawthorne use colors in the book, and for what purpose? What are the colors he uses most often? Give examples of each.

5. What is a symbol? Discuss the range of Hawthorne's symbols, with specific examples.

6. In what different forms does the letter *A* appear?

7. How many important characters appear in the novel? Identify and briefly describe each.

8. Is Hester a Puritan? Is she truly repentant for her sin?

9. Trace the deterioration of Chillingworth. What are his two sins, and what are their effects?

10. Discuss the increasing irony of Dimmesdale's position from the opening scaffold scene until the climax of the novel.

11. Discuss Pearl as a symbol and as a device to work on the consciences of both Hester and Dimmesdale.

12. Which character occupies the central position in the climax of the book? How does this affect the other three characters?

SELECTED BIBLIOGRAPHY

ANDOLA, JOHN A. "Pearl: Symbolic Link Between Two Worlds." *Ball State University Forum* 13 (1972), pp. 60–67.

BAUMGARTNER, ALEX M. and MICHAEL J. HOFFMAN. "Illusion and Role in *The Scarlet Letter.*" *Papers on Language and Literature* 7 (1971), pp. 168-84.

BAYM, NINA. "Passion and Authority in *The Scarlet Letter.*" *New England Quarterly* 43 (1970), pp. 209-30.

BLACK, STEPHEN A. "*The Scarlet Letter:* Death by Symbols." *Paunch* 24 (1965), pp. 51-74.

BOWDEN, EDWIN T. *The Dungeon of the Heart: Human Isolation and the American Novel.* New York: Macmillan, 1961.

BROWNING, PRESTON M. "Hester Prynne as a Secular Saint." *Midwest Quarterly* 13 (1972), pp. 351-62.

COANDA, RICHARD JOSEPH. "Hawthorne's Scarlet Alphabet." *Renascence* 19 (1967), pp. 161-66.

CREWS, FREDERICK. *The Sins of the Fathers.* New York: Oxford University Press, 1966.

CRONIN, MORTON. "Hawthorne on Romantic Love and the Status of Women." *PMLA* 69 (1954), pp. 89-98.

DAVIDSON, EDWARD H. "Dimmesdale's Fall." *New England Quarterly* 26 (1963), pp. 358-70.

DILLINGHAM, WILLIAM B. "Arthur Dimmesdale's Confession." *Studies in the Literary Imagination* 2 (1969), pp. 21-26.

DOUBLEDAY, NEAL F. "Hawthorne's Hester and Feminism." *PMLA* 54 (1939), pp. 825-28.

ELSINGER, CHESTER E. "Pearl and the Puritan Heritage." *College English* 12 (1951), pp. 323-29.

FOGLE, RICHARD H. *Hawthorne's Fiction: The Light and the Dark.* Norman: University of Oklahoma Press, 1952.

GARLITZ, BARBARA. "Pearl: 1850-1955." *PMLA* 72 (1957), pp. 689-99.

GRANGER, BRUCE INGHAM. "Arthur Dimmesdale as Tragic Hero." *Nineteenth-Century Fiction* 19 (1964), pp. 197-203.

HART, JOHN E. "*The Scarlet Letter*—One Hundred Years After." *New England Quarterly* 23 (1950), pp. 381-95.

HAWTHORNE, JULIAN. *Nathaniel Hawthorne and His Wife: A Biography.* Weston, Ontario: R. West, 1973.

HENDERSON, HARRY B. *Versions of the Past.* New York: Oxford University Press, 1974.

HOUSTON, NEAL B. "Hester Prynne as Eternal Feminine." *Discourse* 9 (1966), pp. 230-44.

HUFFMAN, CLIFFORD C. "History in Hawthorne's 'Custom House'." *Clio* 2 (1973), pp. 161-69.

JAMES, HENRY. *Hawthorne.* (English Men of Letters Series) London: Macmillan & Co., Ltd., 1879.

JANSSEN, JAMES G. "Pride and Prophecy: The Final Irony of *The Scarlet Letter.*" *Nathaniel Hawthorne Journal* (1975), pp. 241-47.

KAUL, A. N. "Character and Motive in *The Scarlet Letter.*" *Critical Quarterly* 10 (1968), pp. 373-84.

KHAN, JEMSHED A. "Atropine Poisoning in Hawthorne's *The Scarlet Letter.*" *The New England Journal of Medicine,* 9 Aug. 1984, pp. 414-16.

LAWRENCE, D. H. *Studies in Classic American Literature.* New York: Doubleday Anchor Books, 1955.

LEE, A. ROBERT. *Nathaniel Hawthorne: New Critical Essays.* Totowa, N.J.: Barnes & Noble Books, 1982.

LEVIN, HARRY. *The Power of Blackness.* New York: Knopf, 1958.

MACLEAN, HUGH A. "Hawthorne's *Scarlet Letter:* The Dark Problem of This Life." *American Literature* 27 (1955), pp. 12–24.

MCALEER, JOHN H. "Hester Prynne's Grave." *Descant* 5 (1961), pp. 29–33.

MALE, ROY R. *Hawthorne's Tragic Vision.* Austin: University of Texas Press, 1957.

MCNAMARA, ANNE MARIE. "The Character of Flame: The Function of Pearl in *The Scarlet Letter.*" *American Literature* 27 (1956), pp. 537–43.

O'DONNELL, CHARLES R. "Hawthorne and Dimmesdale: The Search for the Realm of Quiet." *Nineteenth-Century Fiction* 14 (1960), pp. 317–32.

RAHV, PHILIP. "The Dark Lady of Salem." *Partisan Review* 8 (1941), pp. 362–81.

ROPER, GORDON. "The Originality of Hawthorne's *The Scarlet Letter.*" *Dalhousie Review* 30 (1950), pp. 62–79.

SAMPSON, EDWARD C. "Motivation in *The Scarlet Letter.*" *American Literature* 28 (1957), pp. 511–13.

STEINKE, RUSSELL. "The Scarlet Letter of Puritanism." *University Review* 31 (1965), pp. 289–91.

STEWART, RANDALL. *Nathaniel Hawthorne: A Biography.* New Haven: Yale University Press, 1948.

STEPHENS, ROSEMARY. "A is for Art in *The Scarlet Letter.*" *American Transcendental Quarterly* 1 (1969), pp. 23–27.

VAN DOREN, MARK. *Nathaniel Hawthorne.* New York: William Sloane, 1957.

VOGEL, DAN. "Roger Chillingworth: The Satanic Paradox in *The Scarlet Letter.*" *Criticism* 5 (1963), pp. 272–80.

WALCUTT, CHARLES CHILD. "*The Scarlet Letter* and Its Modern Critics." *Nineteenth-Century Fiction* 7 (1953), pp. 251–64.

WALSH, THOMAS F., JR. "Dimmesdale's Election Sermon." *Emerson Society Quarterly* 44 (1966), pp. 64–66.

WENTERSDORF, KARL P. "The Elements of Witchcraft in *The Scarlet Letter.*" *Folklore* 83 (1972), pp. 132–53.

WHITFORD, KATHRYN. " 'On a Field, Sable, the Letter A, Gules.' " *Lock Haven Review* 10 (1968), pp. 33–38.

YOUNG PHILIP, *et al.* Correspondence Section. *New England Journal of Medicine,* 29 Nov. 1984, pp. 1438–41.

—————. *Hawthorne's Secret.* Boston: David R. Godines, 1984.

NOTES

NOTES

NOTES